Ian Boyd John M. Blatt

Investment Confidence and Business Cycles

With 18 Figures

Springer-Verlag
Berlin Heidelberg New York
London Paris Tokyo

Dr. Ian Boyd
GMB Research and Development Pty. Ltd.
Sydney, Australia

Prof. Dr. John M. Blatt
Haifa University
Haifa, Israel

ISBN-13:978-3-642-73120-4 e-ISBN-13:978-3-642-73118-1
DOI: 10.1007/978-3-642-73118-1

Softcover reprint of the hardcover 1st edition 1988

2142/3140-543210

Preface

The aim of this book and a brief description of its contents appear in chapter I. The purpose of this preface is to express our thanks to various people and organizations.

Professor Peter Groenewegen of Sydney University and Dr. Michael Krueger of the University of Massachusetts at Amherst have both been extremely helpful in reading the material and proffering many valuable suggestions. We also wish to thank an anonymous referee for Springer Verlag, for his critical reading and comments. Naturally, we take full responsibility for whatever errors and shortcomings remain.

Our thanks go to Haifa University, particularly the members of the Haifa University Computation Center, for their patience and help in the preparation of the manuscript and production of camera copy. It is a pleasure to acknowledge the assistance of various members of staff of the University of New South Wales, and in particular those at the computer facility within the School of Mathematics.

Ian Boyd, Sydney, Australia
John Blatt, Haifa, Israel.

Table of Contents

CHAPTER I: **Introduction and Brief Summary**

The literature on trade cycles is already enormous, and grows all the time. It is therefore necessary to motivate yet another approach to this well worked area of economics.

For this reason, the first part of this book is historical and critical in nature. The intention is to show that existing approaches to a theory of the trade cycle have serious deficiencies.

In most (though not all) theoretical approaches to the trade cycle, the analysis is carried out entirely in "real" terms, with very little if any attention to "monetary" factors. Indeed, it has become conventional wisdom to think of a "normal trade cycle" as being concerned with real analysis, and to think of a "credit cycle" as something different and perhaps rather exceptional.

We contend that this view is mistaken. The supposed dichotomy between "normal" and "credit" cycles does not exist. The essential features of the observed trade cycle of a laissez-faire system can not be understood in purely real terms. Rather, it is necessary to include the psychological variable of "confidence" with its major effects on credit conditions, and thence on the "real" economy.

In this approach we agree with the school of economists exemplified by Charles Kindleberger and Hyman Minsky. [1] Minsky says "For standard theorists to study the problems of a capitalist economy, they must abandon their normal operating procedure of modelling village fair economies and turn to modelling economies with a Wall Street". [2]

Chapter 2 is devoted to a brief presentation of typical features of the trade cycle of a laissez-faire system. We take mid-nineteenth century Great Britain as our area of main interest. The reasons are explained in chapter 2, and are, briefly: (1) Earlier periods suffer from scarcity of known data, as well as from a greater relative importance of pre-capitalistic features, and (2) Economic conditions at later times have deviated significantly from an ideal laissez-faire system: monopolies, trade unions, state inter-

---

[1] Minsky 1975, 1977; Kindleberger 1982. NOTE: Throughout this book, references to publications are by name of the first author, followed by the year of publication. Co-authors, if any, appear in the list of references at the end of the book.

[2] Minsky 1982 p.16.

vention, currency instability, wars etc. have assumed ever greater importance. The points stressed in chapter 2 are:

1. The importance of credit, speculation and confidence in the course of a typical cycle.
2. The similarities between cycles, as opposed to the detailed differences between the immediate causes of the final breakdown of confidence in different crashes.
3. The asymmetry of the typical cycle: The "ascending phase" takes much more time than the "descending phase", even if one first corrects for the strong upward trend during the nineteenth century.
4. The sheer speed of the "crash" in many cases, with high confidence giving way to a general reluctance to accept anything other than cash on the line, in a matter of months or even weeks.

Chapter 3 is a literature survey of views on the importance of confidence and its fluctuations. The purpose is to show that contemporaries as well as many later observers were well aware of the importance of these factors for an understanding of the phenomenon of the trade cycle.

In chapter 4, we start with a critical discussion of the two main modern theories, namely the theories of the Frisch type (random shocks to a basically stable system) and of the Hicks type (ceilings and floors on a system with an unstable equilibrium). We then summarize, briefly, the arguments [3] which prove that both of these theories are in direct disagreement with the empirical evidence on trade cycles. The chapter closes with a brief section on cycle theories of the type pioneered by Goodwin. [4]

In the case of theories of the Hicks type, the disagreement is well known: Sir John himself was very much aware of the problem. His theory predicts a rapid ascending phase and a much slower descending phase for the cycle, contrary to fact. He suggests, and we agree completely, that one must bring in monetary factors (credit, confidence) in order to overcome this problem.

The situation is different with the second main theoretical approach, the theories of the Frisch type. Such theories are, at present, the conventionally accepted wisdom on the trade cycle. They are believed to agree reasonably well

[3] Blatt 1978, 1980, 1983; Boyd 1986.
[4] Goodwin 1950, 1951, 1955, 1967, 1972.

with trade cycle data, and to give an adequate understanding of the causation of the cycle. We disagree with these claims, emphatically.

Section B of chapter 4 gives a brief summary of the original model of Ragnar Frisch [5] and proceeds to list serious doubts about the mechanism of these models. Section C defines precisely what we mean by "theories of the Frisch type", and summarizes, in non-mathematical terms, a proof that **all** such theories lead to the inescapable conclusion that (after the necessary correction for long term, secular trends) the ascending and descending phases of the cycle must be symmetrical on the average. In particular, if one works from the start with "de-trended" indices, then the average time taken for the upswing must equal the average time taken for the downswing. The mathematical proof is presented briefly in Appendix B. This predicted symmetry between upswing and downswing is in direct contradiction to the data.

Quite apart from the observed asymmetry between the ascent and descent of the cycle, all trade cycle theories couched in purely real terms (the vast majority) encounter major difficulties in explaining the **sheer speed of the crash** in so many cycles. In the nineteenth century, the average length of a major cycle was about 9 to 10 years. Yet, the "crash" often happened in months, or even in weeks. An inescapable difficulty of all "real" theories is that "real" quantities, in particular the stock of real capital, simply cannot change at such precipitate speed. Real capital stock does depreciate, of course, but only over considerably longer periods. On the other hand, psychological quantities such as "confidence" can and do change very rapidly under the influence of mass psychology expressed in market sentiment. Section D of chapter 4 shows how the restriction to "real" quantities influences cycle theories of the Goodwin type.

We conclude that the conventional view of the "normal" trade cycle as being concerned primarily with "real" analysis can not be sustained: (1) It is based on acceptance of theories which are disproved statistically by comparison with observations, and (2) It is incapable of accounting for one of the most striking aspects of actual cycles: the speed of the crash. A valid theory of the trade cycle of a

[5] Frisch 1933.

laissez-faire system must include "psychological" factors right from the start.

This brings us to the second part of the book, in which we motivate and develop a new model of the trade cycle, incorporating an "investor confidence" variable as a major element. This model is not intended as a detailed econometric model; rather, it is akin to the "schematic" models of Hicks or Frisch or Goodwin, i.e., everything is stripped down to the bare essentials, and various rough and ready assumptions are made to simplify the analysis at all stages. There is no intention of a detailed comparison with historical data. Rather, we shall be content if we can get agreement in principle with the asymmetry between ascent and descent, and can account for the speed of the crash.

Chapter 5 provides an introduction to the new model, in relation to evidence from economic history. The essential points of this model are (1) the introduction of an explicit "confidence" variable and (2) the sharp distinction drawn between "real" investment (building of factories, railways, production of machine tools, etc.) and what Joan Robinson [6] terms "placement", meaning the trading of pieces of paper called "shares", "bonds", etc. Note that we reject the pretense that typical owners of shares in a company are in full control of what the company does.

In our model, one "group" of economic actors consists of share buyers who supply the funds with which the second "group" works. This second, quite separate group consists of entrepreneurs engaged in "real" investment in long-term and/or speculative projects.

Chapter 6 explains our treatment of investor confidence. We provide a usable definition of "confidence", by relating it to a variable called the "horizon of uncertainty". This is the time interval over which the typical investor is prepared to place at least some trust in his, or other peoples', predictions of the future.

The horizon of uncertainty is a psychological variable. It contracts sharply when there are shocks to confidence, such as a major bankruptcy. Yet, this psychological variable has major effects on investment evaluation under uncertainty. Let us illustrate this by means of the following **simplified example:** Suppose a project promises a cash flow of one million dollars per annum. If the investor is prepared to believe that this cash flow can be trusted to con-

[6] Robinson 1956 p.6.

tinue five years into the future, then a crude first estimate of its (gross) present value is five million dollars. [7]

On the other hand, suppose the investor is so uncertain of the future that he is not prepared to accept any prediction of future events for more than one year ahead. In that case, the same crude estimate yields a (gross) present value of only one million dollars. [8] This enormous decrease in valuation is brought about by a change in a purely psychological variable, a change which can, and frequently does, spread very rapidly through the money market.

With these preliminaries out of the way, chapter 7 is devoted to a detailed exposition of the new model, providing plausibility arguments for our model equations. Each equation appears at the end of that section in which the equation is motivated and explained. Furthermore, all the model equations are collected together in Appendix C. [9]

The last section of chapter 7 presents some typical computer simulation results with suitably chosen model parameters. These solutions exhibit all the desirable properties of a trade cycle model, as enumerated earlier.

We do not claim that the model gives reasonable results for all values of the parameters. Indeed, the opposite is the case: with unsuitable parameters, the model is entirely capable of generating unrealistic solutions. However, the area of non-linear simulation is so difficult that one should emphasize the existence of parameter sets leading to reasonable solutions, rather than worrying excessively over the existence of other parameter sets. After all, the main modern theories (Hicks and Frisch types) fail utterly to lead to acceptable solutions, no matter how one chooses their parameters.

---

[7] This estimate must be corrected at least for (1) net as against gross present value and (2) the normal discounting of future, as opposed to present, cash flows. However, all these corrections are of only minor importance compared to the main effect, the effect of changes in confidence.

[8] If initial costs of, say, 0.6 million are subtracted to get net values, these values become 4.4 million and 0.4 million dollars, respectively, thus yielding an even larger fractional change in valuations.

[9] Non-mathematical readers may skip the equations, without loss of continuity.

Chapter 8 looks at some longer run (over several cycles) implications, particularly in connection with the money supply.

The closing chapter opens with a section about the economic function of the trade cycle of a laissez-faire market economy. We continue with a section about "exploitation", and we close with some remarks about the implications for current economic theory in general.

Of the mathematical appendices, appendix A contains, in brief outline, a discussion of the statistical proof that the cycle is asymmetric. Although this has been common ground among all economists for over a century, it has been questioned lately, and must therefore be documented in detail. We also comment on some recent, critical papers.

Appendix B outlines the proof that models of the Frisch type necessarily lead to symmetry, on the average, between the ascending and the descending phases of the resulting cycles in de-trended data.

Appendix C contains the equations and the parameter values used for the simulations shown in the last section of chapter 7, and in chapter 8. It is in the nature of the new model that analytic solutions to the model equations are unattainable: The equations are highly non-linear, this non-linearity being both an essential aspect (purely linear equations can be shown to be inadequate for describing a truly endogenous cycle) and the basic cause of the mathematical intractability of the model as a whole.

However, some very interesting partial results can be deduced, and these are summarized in Appendix D. In particular, we show that the model does **not** possess "balanced exponential growth" solutions. In our view the absence of such solutions is a **favorable** point for the model. In spite of their popularity with economic theorists, the empirical evidence is solidly against them: (1) No laissez-faire economy has ever grown in this simple fashion; and (2) All such economies have grown by a series of booms and busts.

Appendix E gives a very brief discussion of our computer simulation methods, some of which are original. None of these appendices give the full mathematical details (see Boyd 1986 for those).

We hope that this brief outline of the contents of this book will help the reader to understand the relationships between the various chapters, and may guide him to the areas of most interest to him.

CHAPTER II: A Brief Historical Survey of the Trade Cycle

In this chapter we introduce what we consider to be the essential features of the observed trade cycle. We start by explaining our reasons for concentrating on the mid-nineteenth century; though we do, on appropriate occasions, include evidence from other periods. Then we examine the conventional classification of cycles, to establish the particular type of cycle (the major cycle) which interests us. We go on to describe, in some detail, the observed features of a particular, but we believe a typical, nineteenth century crash. Finally we extract, from this information, the two main characteristics of observed cycles which we consider to be of outstanding theoretical importance: (1) The asymmetry between slow rise and fast fall; and (2) The sheer speed of the "crash" phase.

SECTION A: WHY THE NINETEENTH CENTURY?

The nineteenth century can be described as the age of laissez-faire capitalism par excellence. The nineteenth century (British) economy was substantially free from earlier state interference and craft guild restrictions, and was not yet modified seriously by the development of various monopolies. Furthermore, at least in England, there was then a stable metallic currency standard.

The effect of government on the economy was minimal, the only exception being protection. Mathias [1] says

> "The state did very little to promote industrial innovation as an act of policy, to stimulate productive investment (except via its military expenditures), to mobilize capital for productive investment" ... "It did not conduct enterprise itself on any scale, certainly not in strategic areas of industrial growth and innovation, limiting its direct commitments to a handful of naval dockyards (producing specialized warships and very active only when new fleets were in commission) and ordnance works such as Woolwich Arsenal." ... "It did not even concern itself much with establishing the usual infrastructure of planning, financ-

---

[1] Mathias 1969.

ing, or organizing the financing of roads, canals, railways or public utilities such as docks." ... "The most important exception to these several generalisations relates to protection. Here the state did set a context which favored the growth of new and rising industries."

Taxation and government spending were very small. Mathias [2] gives, for government expenditure as a percentage of national income the figures in table 2.1.

Table 2.1. BRITISH GOV'T EXPENDITURE AS FRACTION OF G.N.P.

1801 (wartime)	5.8%
1820 (postwar)	3.3%
1850 (peace)	2.4%

No major wars after 1815 interfere seriously with normal economic life. In his chapter on trade cycles, Mathias says

> "From 1815 to 1914, war became an infrequent and minor factor in setting up these pulsations, so that the rhythms inherent in the economic process themselves were dominant. During the Crimean War government spending in the years 1854-6 did outrun income from taxes by over 30 million pounds so a considerable boost was given to the economy in that year, particularly to demand for shipping and the heavy industries."

There was true atomistic competition in most areas of business. Monopolies, oligopolies, trade unions, advertising and trademarks were all weak. Exceptions were the East India Company (ended 1834), the Levant Company's monopoly of trade to the Near East (abolished 1825) and the Bank of England monopoly on issuing bank notes. [3] On trade unions Mathias says: [4]

[2] Mathias 1969 p.41.
[3] Mathias 1969 p.295.
[4] Mathias 1969 p.365.

> "A rapidly expanding labor force, extensive migration and rapidly changing industrial location, as expansion and technical change progressed, weakened the strength and continuity of combinations. With rapidly expanding industries one of the main enemies was the small, newly-established master, undercutting in price, overworking labor, breaking apprenticeship agreements and living, in some cases, more precariously than the skilled journeymen in their societies. This context prevented effective unions altogether amongst unskilled grades."

Throughout the century there was enormous growth, which however was by no means steady. A striking fact about the nineteenth century economies is the titanic upheavals through which they passed. [5]

The instances of commercial panics, booms and busts are too numerous, regular and persistent to be put down to fortuitous coincidence. Such a distinct and prolonged series should not be ascribed to accident. Special explanations for each specific crisis may enable us to understand what causes an unstable, overextended state of the economy to collapse suddenly into wild panic, in each particular crash. However these special explanations fail to show how the economy develops after each panic through periods of prosperity, boom and wild speculation to another unstable overextended state ready to turn again, in an instant, into blind panic. Yet just this is what happened time after time with almost the regularity of waves breaking on a beach. Such movements are what is meant by the term 'trade cycle' (or 'business cycle': we use the terms interchangeably). However, these economic upheavals were of such magnitude that perhaps the term 'cycle' appears too mild. The older and more colorful terminology of the contemporary observers appears more appropriate - boom and bust, upsurge and crisis, panic and collapse.

Our point of view is that the trade cycle is not a mere fluctuation superimposed on a process of steady balanced growth, but is rather an inherent characteristic of a laissez-faire economy. To demonstrate the truth of this assertion, we deliberately choose a historical period in which interferences with the operation of the free market are minimal. Any mechanism which operates independently of such

[5] These are described for example in Hyndman (1892).

interferences must be a basic feature of a free market economy. Nineteenth century trade cycles occurred in the near absence of trade unions, monopolies, wars, unregulated money supply, etc. Thus we can conclude that none of these factors are essential elements of the causation of trade cycles. Some or all of them may modify the operation of the trade cycle in our century, of course, but the basic cause of the cycle must be found elsewhere. To quote Minsky [6] once more:

> "No theory of the behavior of a capitalist economy has merit if it explains instability as the result either of exogenous policy mistakes or of institutional flaws that can be readily corrected. Instability existed long before there was anything now recognized as economic policy, and under a wide variety of banking and financial institutions."

SECTION B: CLASSIFICATION OF CYCLES.

There is general agreement that economic fluctuations are not all of the same type, rather there are different kinds of "cycles". This section contains a brief survey of these classifications. This is well known material, presented here to establish nomenclature and explain what sort of "cycles" we are interested in.

Economic historians [7] [8] [9] distinguish the following main types of cycles:

1. "Minor" cycles, also called Kitchin or inventory cycles, of duration 3 to 3.5 years.
2. "Major" cycles, also called Juglar cycles, of duration 8 to 11 years.
3. "Building" cycles, of duration around 20 years.
4. "Long waves", also called Kondratiev cycles, [10] of duration around 50 years.

---

[6] Minsky 1982 p.16.
[7] Matthews 1959.
[8] Schumpeter 1939 pp.166-171.
[9] Rostow 1948.
[10] Kondratiev 1926.

There is no unanimity about this classification. The identification of the turning points (peaks and troughs) of "major" cycles is in dispute; so is the very existence of building cycles and, particularly, of long waves. Minor cycles are attributed by some [11] to variations in export sales, by others [12] to fluctuations in inventories. There is, however, fairly general agreement that the "minor" cycles represent only a "wave of adaptation" to more fundamental causes, as stated by Metzler: [13]

> "The ultimate cause of cyclical fluctuations must therefore be sought in the investment motives of the business world, or, in other words, in the causes of a fluctuating propensity to invest."

In this book, our main concern is the major cycle. Neither the minor cycles, nor the building cycles, nor the long waves (if any), interest us in what follows.

SECTION C: THE CRASH OF 1873.

Rostow (1948) studied the crisis of 1873 and its aftermath in detail, with reference to statistics of the time. He attributes the severity of that crash to the cessation of investment in foreign countries (e.g. the U.S.A.) by British investors. The flow of capital overseas ceased, and consequently, so did the orders for railway materials from the railway builders: [14]

> "The enormous orders of 1872-73, which had forced the system to full employment and virtually pure inflation, had come from abroad and had centered on the rail-iron trade."

The construction of the American railways was done with British capital, and a very large proportion of the production (e.g. of rails) which went into this construction came from England. The main upturn came in the later part of 1871;

[11] Rostow 1948 p.41.
[12] Metzler 1941, 1946, 1947, 1948; Matthews 1959.
[13] Metzler 1946.
[14] Rostow 1948 p.81.

1872 was a year of great activity in railway construction, and consequently great prosperity in the iron industry. [15]

However, by May 1873 the trade papers reported an almost total shutdown in orders for new rails. [16] The reason becomes apparent when we look to the trade journals. Partington quotes the Iron Age (a trade journal):

> "Three weeks later [from May 8 1873] the Iron Age stated that there had occurred a 'general suspension of railroad building' owing to the inability of the roads to market their securities."

The railroad builders had run out of money, and could not raise more.

Yet, speculators did not seem to read the trade journals, for the price of rails (we mean actual rails, not railway shares) rose from the beginning of 1872 and held its heady level to almost the end of 1873. [17] Furthermore, in spite of the fact that railway construction had stopped, promoters kept floating new companies to construct railway cars for the, now non-existent, railways under construction. [18]

In September 1873, the wave of prosperity ended in one of the worst panics in the history of the United States of America. After the panic came an extended depression. There was no improvement until 1877. Then another cycle started all over again.

The 1873 crash became known universally as the start of the "Great Depression" (until another, even more terrible depression took that title). However, Giffen, writing at that time, doubts this interpretation: [19]

> "The common impression appears to be due to a misinterpretation of two undoubted facts: first, the evident magnitude of the financial collapse in foreign loans, which has been productive of great social distress among the classes who have most ample opportunities of proclaiming their grievances; and next, the

[15] Partington 1929 p.40.
[16] Partington 1929 p.42.
[17] Prices of steel rails month by month are given in table VI, page 232 of Partington 1929. See also: Boyd 1986.
[18] Partington 1929 p.46.
[19] Giffen 1886 p.118.

> magnitude of the decline of foreign trade of the country."

Giffen also suggested that the same sequence of investment boom and crisis would continue, due to the eternal desire of promoters to raise funds: [20]

> "There are reasons in the nature of times of prosperity for the creation of pinchbeck securities, and the details and particular form of security chosen are not of permanent interest. If the class of promoters is checked in one way, they will invent new methods and new fields of deception, still keeping within the wind of any new laws that may be contrived ... Probably promoters will now go into a totally different field, which I am disposed to think will be the creation of trusts."

Note particularly the references to:

1. losing classes with most ample opportunities to proclaim their loss;
2. a class of promoters who will try any method and any "field of deception" to attract investors.

The final sentence of the second quotation shows that Giffen was an extremely perceptive and accurate prophet. In 1877, the year this quotation was published originally, "trusts" were insignificant. The first important "trust" was the Standard Oil Trust, created by John D. Rockefeller (in 1880). [21] Yet, very soon afterwards there began a major wave of formation of "trusts", i.e., large integrated companies which either had a monopoly of some area, or were at least large enough to be effective leaders and price setters in that area, for example John Pierpont Morgan's United States Steel Company. By 1914 it was all over: nearly every major U.S. industry was in the hands of these "trusts"; and so it has remained ever since.

A graph of the level of activity in the speculative industries associated with railway production is instructive. We have chosen to plot the figures for locomotives ordered

---

[20] Giffen 1886 p.131.

[21] LLoyd 1894; Tarbell 1904; Collier 1976 pp.35-38.

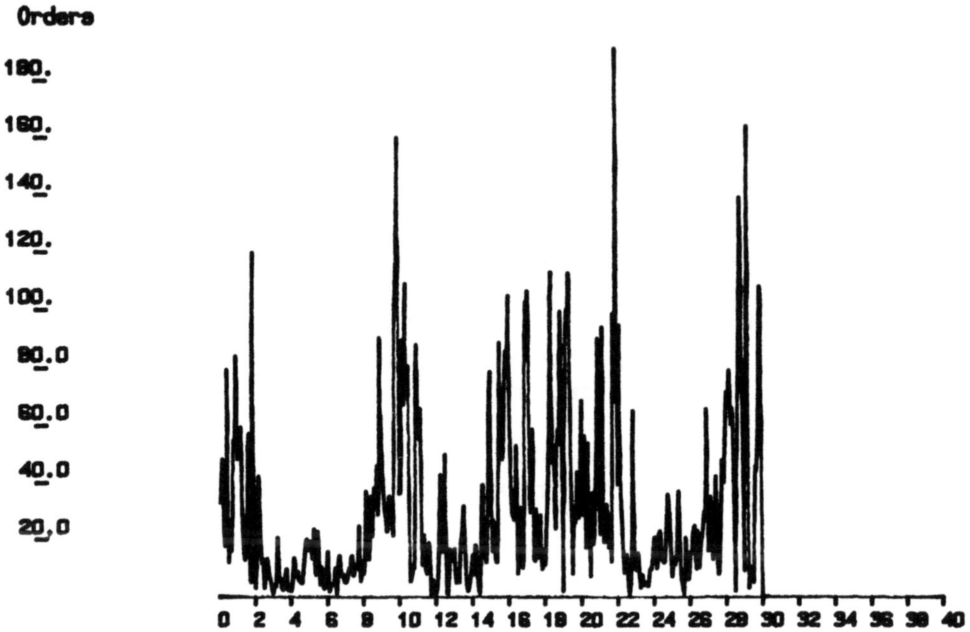

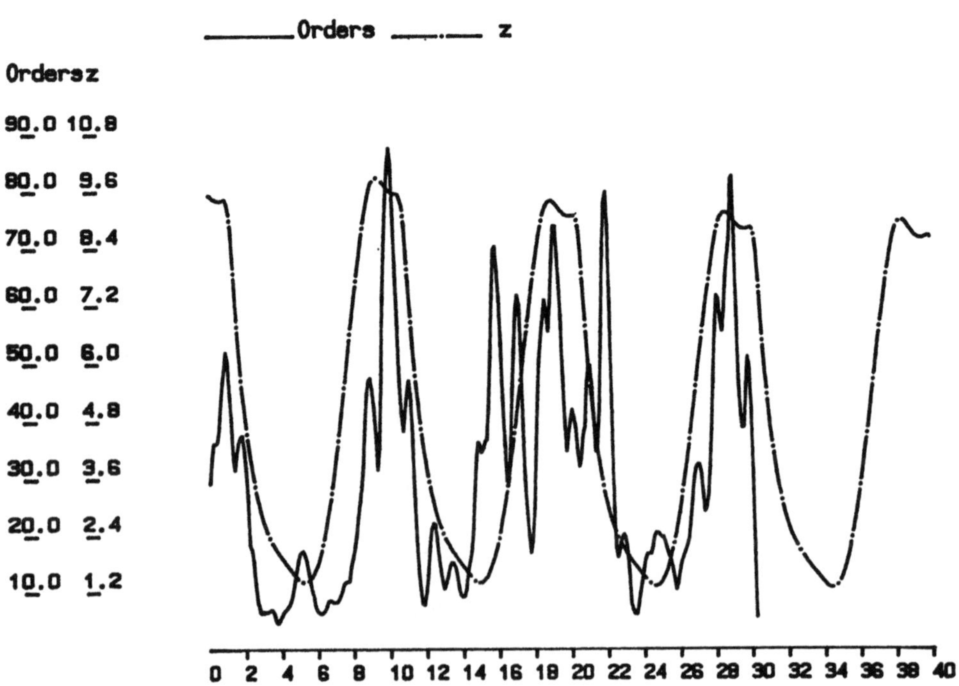

Fig. 2.1. (top): Monthly orders for locomotives from the Baldwin Locomotive Works, from January 1872. Abscissa = years since 1872.
Fig. 2.2. (bottom): Same as Fig. 2.1, but order data smoothed. The dot-dashed curve will be discussed in section 7G.

from the Baldwin Locomotive Works. [22] This is the only large corporation manufacturing railway equipment for which we have access to actual records of orders prior to 1900. [23]

These monthly figures are graphed in figure 2.1. Note that they vary tremendously from month to month. To eliminate some of the violent short term fluctuations, a smoothing technique averaging the raw data over four months before and four months after the point being plotted [24] was used to produce figure 2.2. (The dotted curve in figure 2.2 should be ignored until chapter 7).

The magnitude of the variation in activity is obvious from this graph, the peaks being some 20 times the height of the lowest valley. The swing in "average" levels seems to be about six to one. This figure demonstrates just how violently the actual nineteenth century growth deviated from anything "smooth" or "balanced" or "exponential".

SECTION D: ASYMMETRY BETWEEN RISE AND FALL.

Until quite recently there was universal agreement among economists that the trade cycle exhibits an asymmetry: the rise is comparatively slow, while the fall is extremely rapid. J.K. Galbraith [25] gives a graphic account:

> "The reality in the nineteenth and early twentieth centuries was, in fact, much closer to the teeth of a ripsaw which go up on a gradual plane on one side and drop precipitately on the other. Or, if a wave, it was the long mounting roll and then the breaking surf."

---

[22] The other measures given in Partington, e.g. orders for locomotives, passenger cars, freight cars and rails, all as reported in the trade journals, are too unreliable for our purposes; see Boyd 1986.

[23] Partington 1929 p.11, and table p.227.

[24] See Boyd 1986 for the smoothing technique used.

[25] Galbraith 1975 p.114.

There have been some recent works, however, in which the asymmetry of the cycle has been reinvestigated, [26] or even rejected altogether. [27]

After criticism of earlier methods of data analysis, followed by some extended statistical manipulations, Neftci nonetheless arrives at the universally accepted conclusion:

"... the evidence favors asymmetry." [28]

Quite different are the claims of DeLong and Summers:

"We find no evidence of asymmetry in the behavior of G.N.P. or industrial production. For the U.S. only, we find evidence of some asymmetry in the behavior of unemployment. We conclude that asymmetry is probably not a phenomenon of first order importance in understanding business cycles. It appears that there is not much basis for preferring some version of traditional cyclical techniques of analysis and forecasting to more modern statistical methods." [29]

These claims are startling. However we show, at the end of Appendix A, that they can not be sustained. Using the same data source as DeLong and Summers, and the same basic scheme of analysis, we arrive at diametrically opposite conclusions.

Appendix A contains a detailed analysis of data on U.S. pig iron production (a typical producers' good) from 1877 to 1933. [30]

The outcome of all this analysis is simple and unequivocal: **The hypothesis that the cycle is symmetrical between ascending and descending phases is rejected at a high level of confidence (98 percent). The asymmetry of the cycle is real, not just a statistical artefact.**

---

[26] Neftci 1984.

[27] DeLong 1984, 1986.

[28] Neftci 1984 p.318.

[29] DeLong 1984 p.2.

[30] These are actual data, unlike pre World War I "data" on G.N.P. or unemployment which are later reconstructions. However, the reconstructed G.N.P. values also show the asymmetry, when analysed correctly.

SECTION E: THE SPEED OF THE CRASH.

In his chapter on the trade cycle in "The General Theory", Keynes states: [31]

> "There is, however, another characteristic of what we call the trade cycle which our explanation must cover if it is to be adequate; namely, the phenomenon of the **crisis** - the fact that the substitution of a downward for an upward tendency often takes place suddenly and violently, whereas there is, as a rule, no such sharp turning point when an upward is substituted for a downward tendency."

Any trade cycle theory, to be satisfactory, must exhibit at its upper turning point a sharp peak followed by a precipitate drop, not a gentle curve like a sine wave near its maximum.

As far as the formal definition of a crisis is concerned, Kindleberger and Laffargue [32] summarize the current conventional position as follows:

> "The conference participants occasionally worried how to define a financial crisis: as sharp changes in interest rates, asset prices, or bankruptcy rates (Goldsmith), a threat to the stability of the system (Swoboda), or a rush to test the convertibility of assets into money, or of one money into another (Mundell). No precise agreed definition was reached, but perhaps a financial crisis is like a pretty girl, difficult to define but recognizable when seen. In any event, financial crises were distinguishable from crises of unemployment or crises of wartime devastation and were associated with changed expectations that led owners of wealth to try to shift quickly out of one type of asset into another, with resulting falls in prices of the first type of asset, and frequently bankruptcy."

---

[31] Keynes 1936 p.314.
[32] Kindleberger 1982 pp.1-2.

Marx also refers frequently to the phenomenon of the crisis. He pays particular attention to describing the crash of 1866, as follows: [33]

> "It will be remembered that the year 1857 brought one of the great crises with which the industrial cycle periodically ends. The next termination of the cycle was due in 1866. Already discounted in the regular factory districts by the cotton famine, which threw much capital from its wonted sphere into the great centers of the money-market, the crisis assumed, at this time, an especially financial character. Its outbreak in 1866 was signalized by the failure of a gigantic London Bank, immediately followed by the collapse of countless swindling companies. One of the great London branches of industry involved in the catastrophe was iron shipbuilding. The magnates of this trade had not only over-produced beyond all measure during the overtrading time, but they had, besides, engaged in enormous contracts on the speculation that credit would be forthcoming to an equivalent extent. Now, a terrible reaction set in, that even at this hour (the end of March, 1867) continues in this and other London industries. To show the condition of the laborers, I quote the following from the circumstantial report of a correspondent of the Morning Star, who, at the end of 1866, and beginning of 1867, visited the chief centres of distress: 'In the East End districts of Poplar, Millwall, Greenwich, Deptford, Limehouse and Canning Town, at least 15,000 workmen and their families were in a state of utter destitution, and 3000 skilled mechanics were breaking stones in the workhouse yard (after distress of over half a year's duration) ... I had great difficulty reaching the workhouse door, for a hungry crowd besieged it.'"

A striking example of the sudden violence of the downturn comes from the great crash in 1929, when the valuation of the entire capital stock of the U.S.A. dropped to less than one-half of its original amount in **ten weeks**, between the third of September and thirteenth of November. [34] Even

[33] Marx 1867 pp.625-626.
[34] Galbraith 1955 p.155.

though outside our period, we consider this fantastic drop worth a mention.

The sharp, sudden "crisis" is of great theoretical importance, because it defies explanation by any purely "real" theory. "Real" economic variables, such as the stock of capital, simply can not change that rapidly. Only "monetary" (psychological) variables, such as credit and confidence, can and do change practically overnight. **The very existence of "crises" excludes all purely real theories of the trade cycle (the vast majority) from serious consideration.**

SECTION F: SOME STYLIZED FACTS.

In conclusion, we list here the facts about trade cycles of main interest to us:

1. There exist various types of cycles. The short, minor cycles have been explained as cycles in inventory investment. Doubts continue about the very existence of the 'long waves'. Our interest is in the so called major cycle. We will not include in our model any features leading to minor cycles, nor will we be disappointed if we see no long waves.
2. In the course of a major cycle, investment plays a dominant part. Towards the end of the cycle, speculative investment increases sharply. Important to the fluctuations in investment is investor confidence, or the lack of it.
3. Any satisfactory theory must demonstrate strong asymmetry between the time of rise and the time of fall, with the rise time greatly exceeding the fall time.
4. The phenomenon of the "panic", associated with the speed of the sudden crash at the end of the speculative boom, must also be explained by a satisfactory theory.

CHAPTER III: Literature on Confidence

In this chapter we present an abbreviated literature survey on the importance of confidence and its fluctuations. [1] We intend to show that many economic observers contemporary with the period, as well as later ones, were extremely conscious of the importance of this factor.

We emphasize that our quoting a passage does not imply that we agree or disagree with the economic views of its author, least of all on matters other than investment confidence.

Although "confidence" is used in many different contexts, in this book our main concern is with:

1. The confidence of investors with money to place, in the soundness and future profitability of risky projects whose promoters are looking for investment funds.
2. The confidence of entrepreneurs in these areas, that share or bond issues will attract investment money, not only now but also later on when their projects shall need further injections of funds.

The former is the most important. Although honest, conscientious entrepreneurs are deterred by lack of confidence in the future flow of investment moneys for their projects, quite a few nineteenth century entrepreneurs were neither honest nor conscientious towards their investors. [2]

SECTION A: JOHN STUART MILL.

John Stuart Mill's book 'Principles of Political Economy' [3] summarizes much of the thought of the classical economists. His section "Effects of great extensions and contractions of credit. Phenomena of a commercial crisis analysed" [4] places great emphasis on business confidence and the availability of credit. The crisis is defined as follows: [5]

---

[1] For a fuller survey, consult Boyd (1986).
[2] Josephson 1934.
[3] Mill 1876.
[4] Mill 1876 pp.318-320.
[5] Mill 1876 p.319.

> "There is said to be a commercial crisis, when a great number of merchants and traders at once, either have, or apprehend that they shall have, a difficulty in meeting their engagements. The most usual cause of this general embarrassment, is the recoil of prices after they have been raised by a spirit of speculation intense in degree, and extending to many commodities. ... "
> "When, after such a rise the reaction comes, and prices begin to fall, though at first perhaps only through the desire of the holders to realize, speculative purchases cease: but were this all, prices would only fall to the level from which they rose, ... "
> "To these rational considerations there is superadded, in extreme cases, a panic as unreasoning as the previous overconfidence; money is borrowed for short periods at almost any rate of interest, and sales of goods for immediate payment are made at almost any sacrifice. Thus general prices, during a commercial revulsion, fall as much below the usual level, as during the previous period of speculation they have risen above it: the fall, as well as the rise, originating not in anything affecting money, but in the state of credit."

He blames lack of investment opportunities, and the resulting speculation (mainly in commodities) for the eventual crash: [6]

> "Mines are opened, railways or bridges made, and many other works of uncertain profit commenced, and in these enterprises much capital is sunk which yields either no return, or none adequate to the outlay. Factories are built and machinery erected beyond what the market requires, or can keep in employment ... "
> "By the time a few years have passed over without a crisis, so much additional capital has been accumulated, that it is no longer possible to invest it at the accustomed profit: all public securities rise to a high price, the rate of interest on the best mercantile security falls very low, and the complaint is general among persons in business that no money is to be made ... "

[6] Mill 1876, p.445.

"But the diminished scale of all safe gains, inclines persons to give a ready ear to any projects which hold out, though at the risk of loss, the hope of a higher rate of profit; and speculations ensue."

SECTION B: WALTER BAGEHOT.

Bagehot's "Lombard Street" [7] appeared in 1873, just half a year before the crash described in section 2C. Nowadays, "Lombard Street" is considered, quite rightly, as the first and fundamental treatise on the function and organization of a central bank. Our interest, however, is centered on Bagehot's observations concerning the "panics" of his day. He relates the "lender of last resort" function of the central bank directly to the need to deal with such panics.

Let us see what Bagehot, perhaps the shrewdest economic observer of his time, had to say about the importance of confidence: [8]

"Credit - the disposition of one man to trust another - is singularly varying. In England, after a great calamity, everybody is suspicious of everybody; as soon as that calamity is forgotten, everybody again confides in everybody ... "

"The fact is, that the owners of savings not finding, in adequate quantities, their usual kinds of investments, rush into anything that promises speciously, and when they find that these specious investments can be disposed of at a high profit, they rush into them more and more. The first taste is for high interest, but that taste soon becomes secondary. There is a second appetite for large gains to be made by selling the principal which is to yield the interest. So long as such sales can be effected the mania continues; when it ceases to be possible to effect them, ruin begins ... "

"When we understand that Lombard Street is subject to severe alternations of opposite causes, we should cease to be surprised at its seeming cycles. We

[7] Bagehot 1873.
[8] Bagehot 1873 pp.131, 138-139, 160.

> should cease too to be surprised at the sudden panics. During the period of reaction and adversity, the whole structure is delicate. The peculiar essence of our banking system is an unprecedented trust between man and man; and when that trust is much weakened by hidden causes, a small accident may greatly hurt it, and a great accident for a moment may almost destroy it."

The importance of confidence could hardly be stated more clearly.

SECTION C: ALFRED MARSHALL.

In 1879, Marshall and his wife published a small book called "Economics of Industry". It contained a chapter [9] setting out in clear form his ideas on the trade cycle. Although Marshall in later years said he was not happy with this book, he was referring to other parts of it. His trade cycle theories remained unchanged throughout his life, and that chapter is his clearest statement of them.

Marshall entitled his chapter "Changes In The Purchasing Power Of Money". He was concerned, not only with the problem of recurring panics, but also with the problem of a long term fall in prices, which plagued the British economy particularly at the time this book was written. The first major factor Marshall mentions as affecting prices and economic activity is one which was attracting at the time much attention from other economists, namely gold mining.

> "The most obvious of the causes that affect the purchasing power of the precious metals in a country is the quantity of them that is available for use as money." [10]

However, Marshall quickly overrides this consideration by pointing out that banknotes, checks and bills of exchange form a large part of the money supply, and that fluctuations in these dominate any gold supply fluctuations.

[9] Marshall 1879, Book III, chapter I, pp.150-157.
[10] Marshall 1879.

> "The growth of credit supplies a permanent substitute for the precious metals, and therefore affects their Normal values. But credit fluctuates, and each fluctuation alters their Market values ... "
> "For instance, an expansion of credit coincided with the influx of precious metals consequent on the discovery of the Californian and Australian mines, and increased the upward tendency of prices. But in 1857 there was a crisis; that is, many trading firms were unable to pay their debts, credit was violently contracted, and prices fell, although the store of precious metals in the country was growing as rapidly as ever. After a time credit began to expand again, and prices rose until 1866, when there was another crisis, and prices fell." [11]

Thus, Marshall attributes the changing value of money primarily to the trade cycle with its variations in credit conditions. His view of what happens in such a cycle is:

> "The beginning of a period of rising credit is often a series of good harvests. Less having to be spent in food, there is a better demand for other commodities. Producers find that the demand for their goods is increasing; they expect to sell at a profit, and are willing to pay good prices for the prompt delivery of what they want. Employers compete with one another for labor; wages rise; and the employed in spending their wages increase the demand for all kinds of commodities. New public and private Companies are started to take advantage of the promising openings which show themselves among the general activity. Thus the desire to buy and the willingness to pay increased prices grow together. Credit is jubilant, and readily accepts paper promises to pay. Prices, wages and profits go on rising; there is a general rise in the incomes of those engaged in trade: they spend freely, increase the demand for goods and raise prices still higher. Many speculators seeing the rise, and thinking it will continue, buy goods with the expectation of selling them at a profit. At such time a man, who has only a few hundred pounds, can often borrow from bankers and others the means of buying many thou-

[11] Marshall 1879 p.98.

sand pounds' worth of goods; and every one who thus enters into the market as a buyer, adds to the upward tendency of prices, whether he buys with his own or with borrowed money." [12]

Thus Marshall places great importance on speculation, although he emphasizes speculation in commodities rather than in shares. He continues with the course of the cycle:

"Old firms are borrowing in order to extend their business; new firms are borrowing in order to start their business, and speculators are borrowing in order to buy and hold goods; trade is in a dangerous condition. Those whose business is to lend money are among the first to read the signs of the times, and they begin to think about contracting their loans ... "
"Trading companies of all kinds have borrowed vast sums with which they have begun to build railways and docks and ironworks and factories; prices being high they do not get much building done for their outlay, and though they are not yet ready to reap profits on their investment they have to come again into the market to borrow more capital. The lenders of capital already wish to contract their loans; and the demand for more loans raises the rate of interest very high. Distrust increases, those who have lent become eager to secure themselves; and refuse to renew their loans on easy or even on any terms. Some speculators have to sell goods in order to pay their debts and by doing so they check the rise in prices. This check makes all other speculators anxious and they rush in to sell. For a speculator who has borrowed money at interest to buy goods may be ruined if he holds them a long time even while their price remains stationary; he is almost sure to be ruined if he holds them while their price falls. When a large speculator fails, his failure generally causes that of others who have lent their credit to him; and their failure again that of others ... "
"As credit by growing makes itself grow, so when distrust has taken the place of confidence, failure and panic breed panic and failure. The commercial storm leaves its path strewn with ruin. When it is over

[12] Marshall 1879 p.98-99.

> there is a calm, but a dull heavy calm. Those who have saved themselves are in no mood to venture again; companies, whose success is doubtful, are wound up; new companies cannot be formed. Coal, iron, and the other materials for making Fixed capital fall in price as rapidly as they rose." [13]

We note Marshall's view that confidence, credit and speculation drive the trade cycle. In his (generally strongly supportive) comments on "Say's law", Marshall allows for the following exception:

> "But although men have the power to purchase they may not choose to use it. For when confidence has been shaken by failures, capital cannot be got to start new companies or extend old ones. Projects for new railways meet with no favor, ships lie idle, and there are no orders for new ships ... The chief cause of this evil is want of confidence." [14]

Here again, Marshall declares confidence (or the lack of it) to be the dominant factor.

SECTION D: PIGOU.

Marshall's disciple and successor Professor Pigou gives his own observations on the trade cycle, from which we quote:

> "... We have found, as a dominating cause of trade cycles, wave-like swings in the mind of the business world between errors of optimism and errors of pessimism ..." [15]

In a later work, Pigou states:

> "The activity which is developed in industry under the influence of an error of optimism finally emerges in the form of commodities seeking a market. So long as

[13] Marshall 1879 p.100.
[14] Marshall 1879 p.100-101.
[15] Pigou 1924 pp.96,103.

> these are in process of being created - as we may say, throughout their period of gestation - exceptional activity occurs." [16]

Allowing for the various gestation periods of different investments, before the "test of fact" is applied to their forecast value, nevertheless, in Pigou's view, "When this test has been applied to a fair number of things and found wanting for a fair number, confidence is shaken ...". [17] There follows a general liquidation, and "the dying error of optimism gives birth to an error of pessimism." [18]

Bankruptcies are the operative factor here: "The detonation is greater or less according to the number and scale of the legal bankruptcies into which the detected error explodes." [19]

The failures themselves are not of any material importance - the bankrupt business just passes by sale into the hands of another entrepreneur (in Pigou's observation), but the visibility of bankruptcies breeds fear amongst industrialists that their own debtors may fail.

SECTION E: F. LAVINGTON.

An important work on the trade cycle was published by F. Lavington in 1922. [20] This book describes the cycle and goes on to emphasize the importance of confidence and of speculative price levels. Lavington says [21]

> "In a period of boom, when the causes of business prosperity are imperfectly understood, companies may be floated, and business men may engage in ventures, whose prospective success is estimated less by a rational judgement of the facts than by confidence derived from the visible success of others. And when, in the natural order of events, the inherent weaknesses of the business situation are exposed ... ap-

[16] Pigou 1927 p.83.
[17] Pigou 1927 p.84.
[18] Pigou 1927 p.85.
[19] Pigou 1927 p.86.
[20] Lavington 1922.
[21] Lavington 1922 p.33.

prehension propagates itself cumulatively; and ... a condition of apprehension may rapidly rise to one of panic."

Lavington devotes two whole chapters to studying business confidence. He ties this in closely with price speculation on the commodity and share markets. On page 45 he observes:

> "It is by no means an unimportant matter that a confident view of the future of business should lead speculators to create purchasing power and by its means drive up prices on the Stock and Produce Exchanges".

SECTION F: JOHN MAYNARD KEYNES.

In the chapter on the trade cycle in Keynes "General Theory" everything hinges on the marginal efficiency of capital, which in turn depends on current expectations of future profits.

> "The state of long-term expectation, upon which our decisions are based, does not solely depend, therefore, on the most probable forecast we can make. It also depends on the **confidence** with which we make this forecast - on how highly we rate the likelihood of our best forecast turning out quite wrong. If we expect large changes but are very uncertain as to what precise form these changes will take, then our confidence will be weak.
>
> The **state of confidence,** as they term it, is a matter to which practical men always pay the closest and most anxious attention. But economists have not analysed it carefully and have been content, as a rule, to discuss it in general terms." [22]

Keynes asserts that swings in the marginal efficiency of capital may be much too large to be offset in the short run by interest rate changes. His theory of the crisis is summarized thus: [23]

[22] Keynes 1936 p.148.
[23] Keynes 1936 p.315.

"We have seen above that the marginal efficiency of capital depends, not only on the existing abundance or scarcity of capital-goods and the current cost of production of capital goods, but also on current expectations as to the future yield of capital goods. In the case of durable assets it is, therefore, natural and reasonable that expectations of the future should play a dominant part in determining the scale on which new investment is deemed advisable. But, as we have seen, the basis of such expectations is very precarious. Being based on shifting and unreliable evidence, they are subject to sudden and violent changes ..."
"Now, we have been accustomed in explaining the 'crisis' to lay stress on the rising tendency of the rate of interest under the influence of the increased demand for money both for trade and speculative purposes. At times this factor may certainly play an aggravating and, occasionally perhaps, an initiating part. But I suggest a more typical, and often the predominant, explanation of the crisis is, not primarily a rise in the rate of interest, but a sudden collapse in the marginal efficiency of capital."

J. Maynard Keynes' views clarified significantly during the nineteen thirties. In the General Theory his views were still ambiguous. On the one hand, he gave a supposedly precise formula for the "marginal efficiency of capital". This mathematical expression [24] depends only on (estimated) future cash flows, and therefore makes no **explicit** allowance for uncertainty of the future. On the other hand, throughout the General Theory there is a great deal of discussion of our ignorance of the future, and the effects of this uncertainty on share market valuation of investments. One can not escape the impression that Keynes himself had not, then, succeeded in integrating these two ideas into an organic whole.

However, in his last major theoretical work, [25] Keynes left no doubt whatever about his final position. [26]

"By 'uncertain' knowledge, let me explain, I do not mean merely to distinguish what is known for certain

[24] Keynes 1936 p.135.
[25] Keynes 1937 pp.209-223.
[26] Keynes 1937 p.215.

from what is only probable. The game of roulette is not subject, in this sense, to uncertainty; nor is the prospect of a Victory bond being drawn. Or, again, the expectation of life is only slightly uncertain. Even the weather is only moderately uncertain. The sense in which I am using the term is that in which the prospect of a European war is uncertain, or the price of copper and the rate of interest twenty years hence, or the obsolescence of a new invention, or the position of private wealth-owners in the social system of 1970. About these matters there is no scientific basis on which to form any capable probability whatsoever. We simply do not know. Nevertheless, the necessity for action and for decision compels us as practical men to do our best to overlook this awkward fact and to behave exactly as we should if we had behind us a good Benthamite calculation of a series of prospective advantages and disadvantages, each multiplied by its appropriate probability, waiting to be summed.

How do we manage in such circumstances to behave in a manner which saves our faces as rational economic men? We have devised for the purpose a variety of techniques, of which much the most important are the three following:

1. We assume that the present is a much more serviceable guide to the future than a candid examination of past experience would show it to have been hitherto. In other words we largely ignore the prospect of future changes about the actual character of which we know nothing.

2. We assume that the **existing** state of opinion as expressed in prices and the character of existing output is based on a **correct** summing up of future prospects, so that we can accept it as such unless and until something new and relevant comes into the picture.

3. Knowing that our individual judgment is worthless, we endeavor to fall back on the judgment of the rest of the world, which is perhaps better informed. That is, we endeavor to conform with the behavior of the majority or the average. The psychology of a society of individuals each of whom is endeavoring to copy the others leads to what we may strictly term a **conventional** judgment.

Now a practical theory of the future based on these three principles has certain marked characteristics. In particular, being based on so flimsy a foundation, it is subject to sudden and violent changes. The practice of calmness and immobility, of certainty and security, suddenly breaks down. New fears and hopes will, without warning, take charge of human conduct. The forces of disillusion may suddenly impose a new conventional basis of valuation. All these pretty, polite techniques, made for a well-panelled board room and a nicely regulated market, are liable to collapse. At all times vague panic fears and equally vague and unreasoned hopes are not really lulled and lie but a little way below the surface.

Perhaps the reader feels that this general philosophical disquisition on the behavior of mankind is somewhat remote from the economic theory under discussion. But I think not. Though this is how we behave in the market-place, the theory we devise in the study of how we behave in the market-place should not itself submit to market-place idols. I accuse the classical economic theory of being itself one of these pretty, polite techniques which tries to deal with the present by abstracting from the fact that we know very little about the future."

Shackle has this to say about this famous passage:

"Keynes' expositors, commentators and critics either contrive, for the sake of their peace of mind, to leave this passage unread, or else they turn aside as men who have looked over the edge into the abyss and must endeavor to blot this dreadful vision from their mind. For this passage pronounces the dissolution of the view of business conduct as rational, as the application to men's affairs of fully-informed reason. Yet it is the assumption that men act by fully-informed reason that underlies the whole of value-theory; that underlies what, until forty years ago, was virtually the whole of economic theory ..." [27]

Keynes' quote is from 1937, Shackle's comment from 1974. Let us add that the "Keynesian counter-revolution" has made

[27] Shackle 1974 p.38.

these quotations ever more apposite and timely, year by year.

SECTION G: HYMAN MINSKY.

Minsky starts from his interpretation of Keynes. This leads him to a theory in which investment decisions in financial instruments are the key determinants of aggregate real and financial activity.

> "In his rebuttal to Viner, Keynes insisted that the main propositions of the 'General Theory' center around the disequilibrating forces that operate in financial markets. These disequilibrating forces directly affect the valuation of capital assets relative to the prices of current output, and this price ratio, along with financial market conditions, determines investment activity. The 'General Theory' is thus concerned with how these two sets of prices (capital and financial assets on the one hand, and current output and wages on the other) are determined in different markets and by different forces in our economy, and why such an economy is 'so given to fluctuations'." [28]

One of the aspects of Keynes' theory emphasized by Minsky is the role of uncertainty and confidence:

> "In Keynes' theory, 'time' is calendar time and the future always is uncertain. Thus investment and financing decisions are made in the face of intractable uncertainty, and uncertainty implies that views about the future can undergo marked changes in short periods of time. In particular, changing views of the future affect the relative price of various capital assets and financial instruments, as well as the relation between capital-asset price and the price of current output." [29]

[28] Minsky 1977 p.6.
[29] Minsky 1977 p.8.

Minsky contends that to understand the capitalist economy, finance must be introduced and the cash flows and interrelated balance sheets of the economic entities must be examined explicitly. [30] Compared to cash flows and financial asset positions, he considers commodities and their markets to be of secondary importance. Minsky views the economy as consisting of a set of balance sheets in which assets generate cash receipts and liabilities state payment commitments. [31]

He subdivides the financial entities (balance sheets) into several classes. The first, which he calls "hedge finance", anticipate cash flows from their operations large enough to meet all future payment commitments on debts. A second, "speculative finance", has cash flows from operations which are not expected to meet payment commitments fully. [32] Later, he introduces a special kind of speculative finance called "Ponzi finance", named after a Boston swindler.

Minsky's example of a "hedge finance" entity is a normal trading or manufacturing firm. An example of a "speculative finance" entity would be a trading bank or finance company. A "Ponzi finance" entity is characterized by yielding no revenues at all until after the project has been finished.

Minsky has been criticized for his use of these terms. The term "speculative" for activities as widespread and apparently sound as the business of a savings bank, and "Ponzi finance" to describe such operations as loan financed building construction has been called "irresponsible". [33] However, the basic ideas of Minsky remain unaffected by criticisms of his terminology.

Minsky's financial instability hypothesis is that an initially stable financial system, consisting largely of "hedge finance" units, gradually becomes transformed, over a run of good years, into one dominated by speculative and "Ponzi finance" units. Thus stability is itself destabilizing. [34]

Minsky's cycle model proceeds as follows: Investment goods financing conforms to "Ponzi finance"; an investment boom leads to higher short term and long term interest rates and also leads to the finance system being heavily weighted

---

[30] Minsky 1982 p.13.
[31] Minsky 1982 p.20.
[32] Minsky 1977 p.13.
[33] Goldsmith 1982 p.43.
[34] Minsky 1982 pp.24-27.

by speculative and "Ponzi" finance. The higher interest rates result in negative present values of some "Ponzi" financed investment, which leads to failure of these ongoing investment projects to obtain the cash needed for their completion. This gives rise to finance problems for lenders and a need for them to acquire cash by sale of other financial assets. These sales force a rapid fall in prices of these financial assets, decreasing investment and cutting profits. [35] To Minsky, therefore, the upper turning point is completely endogenous.

The lower turning point is attributed to a process of debt deflation leading to a (temporarily) more stable system. In modern economies, Minsky says, the lender of last resort can also initiate the lower turning point. [36] Minsky's lower turning point is more a floor than a sharp turn.

SECTION H: CONCLUSION.

In this chapter we have quoted a few of the many observers who have pointed out the importance of confidence and its fluctuations. Some lived in the period which we are studying, others are much more recent. Based on these opinions, it would seem reasonable that a model of the trade cycle should incorporate confidence right from the start.

[35] Minsky 1982 pp.32-33.
[36] Minsky 1982 p.33.

CHAPTER IV: The Dominant Theories

This chapter is addressed to the main modern theories of the trade cycle, showing that these theories, which are couched in purely "real" terms, do not fit the facts. In the case of the most widely accepted theory, that the economy is fundamentally stable but subject to random shocks, we go into some statistical and mathematical detail.

SECTION A: HICKS TYPE THEORIES.

Although conventional economic models are usually not strictly linear, the non-linearities which occur are generally "mild". For example, there may be a reduction to "constant prices", amounting to division of a total cost C by some price index P: C/P. [1] Mathematically speaking, such a term is non-linear. However, unless the economy is going through a hyper-inflation, non-linearities of this sort are in the nature of minor corrections; they do not alter the overall pattern of possible solutions to a significant extent. We shall refer to models of this sort as "essentially linear".

Linear economic models have a very limited repertoire of possible solution types. Ignoring (as we should) certain very special cases which arise only through accidental relationships between the model parameters, there are only four types:

1. Exponentially increasing solutions.
2. Oscillations with exponentially increasing amplitude.
3. Oscillations with exponentially decreasing amplitude.
4. Exponentially decreasing (without oscillations).

The most general solution of a linear model consists of a linear superposition of one or more of these four types of behavior.

---

[1] See for example: (1) the London Business School Model of the U.K. Economy; (2) the U.K. Treasury Short-Term Forecasting Model; (3) the Southhampton Econometric Model of the U.K. and its Trading Partners; all in Renton 1975.

Paul Samuelson [2] first suggested a "multiplier accelerator" model of a growing cyclical disturbance (linear in his first paper, non-linear but essentially linear in our sense in the second paper.) The linear model gives rise to oscillations for a wide range of model parameters. These oscillations grow with time if the "accelerator constant" v exceeds unity, they die down with time if v is below unity.

The two main modern theories are logical developments of these two alternatives. [3] If the parameter v is assumed to be below unity, then the model economy has a stable (growth) equilibrium. The "Frisch type models" start from this assumption. It is then necessary to think of a mechanism to keep oscillations going (since they would die down of their own accord otherwise). "Random shocks" are the mechanism assumed by Frisch type models. Such models will be discussed in later sections of this chapter, and in Appendix B.

The second alternative is to assume a value of v in excess of unity, which means an unstable equilibrium for the model economy. The Samuelson mechanism then gives rise to oscillations with increasing amplitude. However, it does not take long before these oscillations become so large as to be economically impossible (for example, until national income becomes negative over part of the model cycle). Thus, the model must be modified, to limit the size of these oscillations. This second path was taken by Sir John Hicks. He stated his position as follows: [4]

> "It is possible that the investment coefficient may be, at least as a rule **above** its middle point. [In our terms: v may be above unity.] At first sight, this alternative looks quite ridiculous; one's first reaction is to reject it out of hand. For if the investment coefficient lies above the middle point, the cycles produced by a single shock will be explosive ... But suppose there is some constraint which prevents the fluctuations from passing outside certain limits; the system might then continue periodically

---

[2] Samuelson 1939, 1939a.

[3] Logical, but not historical. The Frisch suggestion of a stable economy subject to random shocks was made six years before Samuelson's papers.

[4] Hicks 1950 pp.91-92.

breaking its head against these limits without running away altogether."

Hicks pointed out that certain common sense limits must apply. In an actual economy investment cannot go very negative, since gross investment must be positive and thus net investment cannot be more negative than allowed by depreciation. In the other direction, production and consumption are limited by available land, population size, capacity of mines etc.

Hicks' resulting model equations are non-linear in the mathematical sense; the non-linearity operates whenever a ceiling or floor is reached. The equations remain linear between the ceiling and the floor.

The Hicks model gives rise to regular cyclical behavior. However Hicks himself criticizes his model for the unacceptable shape of this cycle: [5]

"What, however, of the downswing? Here at once we get into difficulties. One of the most striking characteristics of actual cycles is that output, once it has passed its peak, falls off rather rapidly. This does not happen invariably (and on our theory we do not expect that any particular property, such as this, of the actual cycle will be invariable); but it has happened sufficiently often for it to seem likely that a **rapid** downswing ought to be a feature of the theoretical cycle, if we are on the right lines. ... On our theory we do not get a rapid downswing."

Hicks suggests that his basic model is sound but that some other mechanism is needed to speed up the fall:

"What we have been showing is that the cycle itself, regarded as a periodical fluctuation in output, can be explained in terms of simple reactions, by entrepreneurs and by consumers, which are not in any mysterious sense psychological, but are based on the technical necessities of a capital using economy. But we are not obliged to maintain that all aspects of the cycle can be explained in these terms. It would be surprising, for instance, if the price mechanism and

[5] Hicks 1950 p.90.

> the monetary mechanism, about which we have said little or nothing had no part to play in the story." [6]

Throughout his book Hicks attempts to explain the main features of the cycle in purely real terms. [7] It is only in response to his failure to fit the slow rise fast fall criterion that he concedes a role for the price and monetary mechanism. However, once forced into this necessity Hicks links the speed of the fall with financial matters - liquidity preference, financial crises:

> "Here it is only necessary to suggest that the same forces of 'liquidity preference' which are evidently responsible for the association of cyclical downturn with financial crises, can very plausibly be involved to explain the rapidity of the downswing." [8]

Our point of view has many points of contact with Hicks'. The main difference is one of emphasis. We agree that the "balanced growth path" is inherently unstable (though not necessarily for the reasons given by Hicks), and thus actual growth is not normally balanced. We agree emphatically that "monetary" factors (credit, confidence, etc.) must be brought in; however, we feel they should be brought in right from the start, rather than as an afterthought grafted onto a basically "real" theory.

SECTION B: FRISCH TYPE THEORIES.

In 1933, at the dismal low point of the "Great Depression", Ragnar Frisch published a famous paper called "Propagation and Impulse Problems in Dynamic Economics". He starts with a linear model, different in detail (but not in principle) from the accelerator multiplier model of Samuelson. This linear model is capable of giving oscillations. However, Frisch chooses model parameters for which these oscillations are damped, so they die out eventually. He remarks: [9]

---

[6] Hicks 1950 p.117.
[7] Hicks 1950 p.136.
[8] Hicks 1950 p.117.
[9] Frisch 1933 p.197.

"The examples we have discussed in the preceding sections, and many other examples of a similar sort that may be constructed, show that when an economic system gives rise to oscillations, these will most frequently be damped. But in reality the cycles we have occasion to observe are generally not damped."

Frisch proposes that a separate mechanism, which he calls "impulse", is needed in order to keep the oscillation going. This mechanism consists of erratic shocks to the model; and he produces manually calculated simulations to support this idea.

The concept of separate "impulse" and "propagation" problems derives from an earlier suggestion by Wicksell: "If you hit a wooden rocking horse with a club, the movement of the horse will be very different to that of the club." [10]

Let us now list some salient points, and some basic criticisms, of the Frisch mechanism:

1. The inherent motion of the system (the "propagation problem") consists of damped oscillations, i.e., the equilibrium around which the system oscillates is **stable.** This is an essential point of difference from the Hicks model.
2. A separate mechanism (the "impulse") is needed, and is therefore assumed, in order to keep the system from settling down permanently into its 'natural' state of equilibrium.
3. Frisch's examples of damped systems are purely theoretical, and there is no difficulty in constructing other examples in which the cycles are undamped. Indeed, this is precisely what Samuelson did some six years later. Thus, the assertion "when an economic system gives rise to oscillations, these will most frequently be damped" has not been proved. On the contrary, reasonable estimates of the investment coefficient v for actual economies lead to the very opposite conclusion: an unstable equilibrium (v exceeds unity).
   The undoubted truth is: "When an economic system gives rise to oscillations, these are normally limited in size and do not grow beyond all bounds." If the economic system can be described validly by a **linear** model, then the second statement implies the first: in a linear

[10] Wicksell, as quoted by Frisch 1933 p.198.

model, oscillations can be limited only by means of (linear) damping. However, there is no reason whatever to assume that actual economies are linear systems; the oscillations of **non-linear** systems are often limited in size by the non-linearity (for example, the ceiling and floor in the Hicks model) rather than by a simple damping mechanism.

4. The simile of the "rocking horse" is worth a closer look. A rocking horse is hardly the most usual piece of furniture. If one hits, in a random manner, an ordinary table or chair, then the resulting motions are really rather similar to the originating impulses. The rocking horse is different, because it is a very special system, namely one with an extremely weakly damped natural oscillatory motion. In non-technical terms: if one starts a rocking horse going, then its "natural tendency" is to keep on oscillating for quite a long while, in a regular manner, taking a considerable time to settle back to rest. **The Frisch mechanism depends on this special property.** Without it, the system subject to the impulses moves in a way fairly similar to the impulses, not at all in a nearly regular oscillatory manner. Thus, a rather special and quite implausible property of the economic system must be **assumed** before the Frisch mechanism can operate in the intended manner.
5. An important point concerns the **magnitude** of the oscillations induced by the shocks. If and only if the investment coefficient v is very close indeed to (and just slightly below) unity, then shocks of reasonable size give rise to oscillations of acceptable amplitude. If this condition is not true - and there is no reason to assume that it is true for actual economies - then, although shocks still drive the system into apparent oscillations, the size of these oscillations remains minute, so that the oscillations are hardly noticeable. [11]

---

[11] The mathematics of this would carry us too far here. If the shocks are "random", then the state of affairs is similar to that in a "random walk". If a drunken man takes steps at random, forward and backward, he does not, except in very rare cases, move very far from his starting point. An oscillation "driven" by such a random walk does not, on the average, build up much amplitude.

This is the mathematical reason behind the common finding that exogenous shocks of reasonable size do **not** give rise to acceptable results. Zarnovitz and his collaborators simulated four large models of the United States economy, using actual past data for the exogenous variables, to see how well these models could fit the past behavior of the economy. They found: [12]

> "common to both short and long non-stochastic simulations is a strong tendency to underestimate the amplitudes of the observed cyclical movements".

A similar investigation by I. and F. Adelman of a model of the U.S. economy, but using randomly fluctuating exogenous variables, also produced cycles of insufficient amplitude. [13]
We conclude that, with the best available econometric models, **shocks to the exogenous variables can at most be a small part of the reason for cycles of the observed magnitude.**

6. As a result of the insufficient size of the oscillations, the assumed nature of the "shocks" initiating them has, of necessity, been altered considerably from the original notion of Frisch. Rau has this to say on the nature of the shocks: [14]

> "The shocks which appear to be crucial are the disturbance terms in the structural equations of the models: in other words, the random components in the relations determining the endogenous variables; in the model used by the Adelmans, these random components were most important in the equations determining fixed investment and business saving. These shocks may be interpreted as evidence of the importance of unpredictable and unsustained changes in mood or taste within the private sector, or as an indication that the model itself has failed to take into account some important feature of the economy."

[12] Zarnovitz 1972 p.527.
[13] Adelman 1959.
[14] Rau 1974 p.68.

This is a grave admission: We must accept either (1) "unpredictable and unsustained [and, we may add, unexplained] changes in mood and taste", or (2) admit that "the model has failed to take into account some important feature of the economy". This is hardly an inviting choice.

7. Our last point concerns the **shape** of these oscillations. In the absence of further impulses, the 'propagation' oscillations are damped sine waves. Such waves are symmetrical between ascent and descent. When random impulses continue to impact the system, the waves are modified considerably.
However the main features are preserved, particularly as regards the **average** behavior of the oscillations. This remains symmetrical between ascent and descent (we shall discuss this in detail, in section C of this chapter, and in Appendix B). This theoretically expected property is **contrary** to what is observed in actual trade cycles (see section 2D and appendix A).

Thus, the Frisch mechanism not only depends for its action on highly implausible assumptions about the underlying economy (investment coefficient v very close to, and slightly below, unity) and about the "shocks" to it (unpredictable and unsustained changes in mood and taste within the private sector), but even under these unlikely assumptions it gives "cycles" which differ significantly from what is observed.

In view of these serious defects, it may appear highly surprising that the Frisch mechanism has been accepted so widely as the standard, conventional explanation of the trade cycle. [15] For example, Rau [16] has summarized the majority position in these words:

"What are we to conclude from this survey of models? At first it does seem that deterministic income expenditure models which generate oscillations that are unstable, only slightly damped, or constrained as in the ceiling floor model, do **not** give a plausible explanation of the quantitative feature of cyclical be-

---

[15] Wesley Mitchell never did accept it - he had a healthy respect for the data, and took it for granted that the cycle was basically endogenous in origin.
[16] Rau 1974 pp.67-68.

havior in advanced economies. This does not, of course, rule out the possibility that theoretical models, involving no shocks, may give a plausible explanation of long swings; similarly it may be true that radically new insights may give a better explanation of the short cycle than anything discussed in this book. What does seem to be correct is that, given our existing corpus of macro-economics, the picture of a fundamentally stable system subject to random shocks is more accurate than that of a highly unstable system with or without them."

It appears likely to us that the well-nigh universal acceptance of the Frisch mechanism is related, at least to some extent, to an overall "philosophical" attitude of many economists. This attitude is one of opposition to government interference with the free market and therefore disapproval of any economic theory which could possibly be used to justify such interference.

If one accepts that the economy is of the Hicks type, with an unstable equilibrium and a tendency to continue "breaking its head" against ceilings and floors, then one might well be tempted to conclude that a wise government should interfere with this 'natural' tendency, by means of some stabilisation scheme.

By contrast, a Frisch economy has a stable equilibrium, so that market forces tend to push the economy back to this equilibrium of their own accord. Stabilisation of a Frisch economy would require elimination of all random shocks, which looks like a pretty hopeless task. Thus, on both these grounds, the Frisch mechanism supports the case for non-interference. We suggest that it is considerations of this sort, probably largely subconscious, which underlie the present, almost universal acceptance of the Frisch mechanism.

SECTION C: DISPROOF OF FRISCH TYPE MODELS.

In this section, we elaborate on the final point of criticism (point 7) of Frisch type models in the preceding section: The **shape** of the cycle is predicted to be symmetrical between upswing and downswing, on the average, whereas actual observed cycles are clearly asymmetrical.

We consider this argument conclusive against all models of the Frisch type. Since the details of the argument are in the literature, [17] we only give an outline of the salient points here.

A. The economic variables of the models we work with are logarithmic (plotted on a "ratio scale"). For example, we consider the logarithm of the rate of production of pig iron, not the rate of production itself; and similarly for other variables. This is conventional practice in present day model building. [18]

For our purposes, there is an additional, compelling reason for choosing logarithmic variables. In investigating trade cycles, we are forced to consider time intervals containing many cycles. In such long time intervals, the general upward trend of all economic indices can not be ignored. Without ratio scales (logarithms), the large values toward the end of the time interval would dominate all the statistics for the entire time interval. [19]

For this reason, our variables are logarithmic. A deviation of, say +0.01, means 1 percent more than the long term trend, while -0.01 means 1 percent less than the trend; etc.

B. "Models of the Frisch type" are defined in analogy to Frisch's basic idea, but so as to include nearly all the actual models used by econometricians. The defining properties are:

1. In the absence of shocks, the "natural motion" of the model must be stable. That is, there must be a natural tendency to approach some smooth growth path, which does not itself exhibit business cycle type ups and downs.
2. The random shocks which push the model away from its trend path must be sufficiently small so that the devi-

[17] Blatt 1980; Boyd 1986.

[18] See, for example, Jonson 1977.

[19] It is possible to avoid this by making ad hoc statistical assumptions about time varying correlation matrices (heteroscedasticity). However, ratio plots are much simpler and straightforward, besides having an underlying economic rationale: Increasing production by a certain ratio, say by 10 percent, involves nearly the same effort, no matter what the base from which we start.

ations from trend can be treated to sufficient accuracy by an approximation linear in these deviations. [20]

3. The statistical distribution of the random shocks must exhibit the following **symmetry property:** Let there be a certain probability, call it P, of getting a particular series of shocks [q(1), q(2), ..., q(T)] at times t=1, t=2, ..., t=T. Then the probability of getting the **reversed** series of shocks: [-q(1), -q(2), ..., -q(T)] is exactly the same, i.e. it is also equal to P. In other words, if the direction of every shock of the series is reversed (upward shocks are replaced by downward shocks of the same size, and vice versa), then this new series of shocks has the same probability as the original series.

Any model which satisfies these three conditions is a "Frisch type model" for our purposes. All commonly used econometric models do satisfy these conditions, and are therefore Frisch type models in our sense. [21]

C. In analysing cycles, it is necessary to have rules for identifying the "peaks" and "troughs" of economic time series. [22] The raw data are very "jagged", and thus the "turning point identification rules" of the N.B.E.R. turn out to be quite complicated. [23] However, all we need for our proof is another **symmetry property.**

Suppose we have an economic time series [y(1), y(2), ..., y(T)] representing deviations from a smooth trend path. If

---

[20] This condition sounds more stringent than it actually is. Linearity is **not** required for the trend path itself (i.e., this path need not be a simple balanced exponential growth). Linearity is assumed only for the small deviations around the trend path.

[21] An exception is a recent proposal by Neftci 1984, see p.325. Neftci proposes "innovations [which] have asymmetric densities" in order to save, we feel by a desperate last ditch effort, the linearity and stability of the underlying model economy. This appears to be a case of allowing the desire for mathematical simplicity to dictate model building, at the expense of economic realism.

[22] This is denied by DeLong and Summers (1984), who suggest analysing the raw data. See appendix A for a criticism of this proposal.

[23] Bry 1971.

the trend curve has been chosen correctly, then the deviations y(t) have mean value zero. We analyse this series by whatever turning point rules we decide to adopt, and thus locate cyclical peaks and troughs for this de-trended series.

Now consider the **reversed** series [-y(1), -y(2), ..., -y(T)], in which every excess has been turned into a deficiency, and vice versa. [24] Let us apply our turning point identification rules to this reversed series, also. The symmetry property we demand (and which is actually satisfied by the turning point identification rules of the N.B.E.R.) is that the rules should be symmetrical between identifying a peak and a trough. That is, the same turning points should be identified for the two series postulated above, with the peaks of the original series becoming troughs of the reversed series, and vice versa.

D. It is worthwhile, at this stage, to point out certain features which do **not** enter our proof and therefore do not affect our conclusions:

1. Our conclusions are independent of the **size** of the econometric model, i.e., of the number of endogenous variables in the model. All we require are the postulated reflection properties; once they are granted, the conclusions are as true of a monster model with thousands of variables, as of a mini model with less than two dozen variables.
2. Our conclusions do **not** depend on some assumed lack of auto-correlation between the shock terms of the model. Let the shocks be correlated in any way whatever. All we require for our conclusions is that a time series of shocks and its reversed series should always occur with the same probability. For example, if a positive shock at time t is correlated with a positive shock at time t+1, then we require that a negative shock at time t be equally correlated with a negative shock at time t+1.

---

[24] Note that this operation is not reversal of the sense of time (this would mean replacing t by T-t); rather, it is reversal of upward fluctuations by downward fluctuations, and vice versa. Conventional econometric models are not invariant under time reversal; but linearized models **are** invariant under the reflection envisaged here, i.e., they do have our postulated reflection property.

E. We are now in a position to state our fundamental **symmetry theorem:**

> Let the econometric model be of Frisch type; and let the rules used for determining turning points for each economic variable satisfy our reflection invariance. Then it is true that any given set of upslopes and downslopes, and its "reversed" set (upslopes turned into downslopes, and vice versa) must have exactly the same probability of being realized.

The proof of this theorem is given in appendix B. The underlying idea is quite simple. Take any realization of the time series which leads to a certain set of slopes. Now carry out a "reflection" on this time series pattern, i.e. replace every deviation y(t) by its negative, -y(t). By the reflection property for a Frisch type econometric model, the reflected time series occurs with the same probability as the original one. By the reflection property for turning point identification rules, the same turning points are identified, but with opposite sense (peaks become troughs, and vice versa). Since the slopes are obtained by drawing straight lines between peaks and adjacent troughs, exactly the same slopes are obtained as before; but what was the slope of an ascending phase now becomes the slope of a descending phase, and vice-versa. Thus, if the original time series led to a certain set of upslopes and downslopes, then the reflected series leads to the reversed pattern (upslopes have become downslopes, and vice versa); furthermore, both these time series occur with exactly equal probability. Since **all** time series realizations of the model can be so paired, the conclusion of the theorem follows. Thus, there **should be full symmetry between ascending and descending slopes if the Frisch theory is true.**

F. It is shown in Appendix B that our fundamental symmetry theorem leads to the following corollaries for all Frisch-type models:

1. Let r'(n) be the average of the first n ascending slopes; and let r"(n) be the average of the first n descending slopes, for some economic variable. Then the statistics r'(n) and r"(n) are distributed identically.
2. In particular, the expected value of r'(n) equals the expected value of r"(n).

3. The statistic x defined by $x=[r'(n)-r''(n)]/[r'(n)+r''(n)]$ is distributed symmetrically around x=0, with the expected value of x being zero.

G. Our symmetry theorems and corollaries are assertions about the consequences of the Frisch theory of business cycles. Let us now compare these predictions with observations of actual economic behavior, as summarized in Burns and Mitchell. [25]

We require average values of ascending and descending slopes, after removal of long-term trend factors, for a number of typical economic time series. Just such values are given by Burns and Mitchell, in their table 97 on page 291. Below, we reproduce an extract from this table, in which we concentrate on "corresponding" cycles, i.e., cycles which appear both in the original, and in the trend-adjusted, data.

Table 4.1. AVERAGE UPSLOPES R'(N) AND DOWNSLOPES R"(N) FOR A NUMBER OF ECONOMIC TIME SERIES (FROM BURNS AND MITCHELL).

Series	No. of cycles (n)	r'(n)	r"(n)	x
Deflated clearings	13	0.64	1.93	-0.502
Frickey's clearings	9	0.69	1.65	-0.420
A.T. & T. index	9	1.12	1.79	-0.230
Pig iron production	15	2.49	4.02	-0.235
Electricity output	2	0.48	0.69	-0.179
Railroad bond yields	16	0.62	0.65	-0.024

The expected values of r'(n) and r"(n) should be equal, on the Frisch theory. The observations summarized in Table 4.1 are in clear contradiction to this expectation. With the exception of railroad bond yields, the average upward slope r'(n) is appreciably below the value of the average downward slope r"(n), for all these series. The disparity appears particularly in the indices of bank clearings, and is still very pronounced in the (wider-ranging) A.T.&T. index of business activity, as well as in pig iron production.

[25] Burns 1947.

Electricity output, though based on only two full cycles, is a particularly interesting case. In the U.S.A., electricity production had a strongly rising trend during the years covered in this table. Before elimination of this trend, one gets [26] r'(n)=0.97, r"(n)=0.80, i.e. the upward slope appears steeper than the downward slope. But this is due purely to the long term trend; when this trend is removed from the data, the figures are as listed in the Table, with upward slope considerably less than the downward slope. [27]

However, there are bound to be some who question the statistical significance of this comparison. Our theorems guarantee that the expected values of r'(n) and r"(n) are equal to each other; but they do not guarantee the same for the actual values. Conceivably, the asymmetry so evident in table 4.1 could be the result of a mere statistical fluctuation. It is necessary, therefore, to attempt to assess the probability of a fluctuation of this enormous magnitude. This matter is discussed in Appendix B.

The conclusion reached in Appendix B is that, for the data on pig iron production in the U.S.A. between 1877 and 1933, the likelihood of such an enormous fluctuation is extremely small (confidence level of 98 percent that the set of upslopes and the set of downslopes can not arise from the same underlying distribution). Furthermore, we are convinced that this confidence level can be improved considerably by more detailed analysis, if wanted.

We conclude that all Frisch type theories of the business cycle are in direct contradiction with the observations.

SECTION D: GOODWIN TYPE MODELS.

For many years, Richard Goodwin [28] has pioneered an alternative type of model, which attempts to put into mathematical form some of the ideas of Karl Marx on the

---

[26] Burns 1947 p.291.
[27] Note that this is a counterexample to, and hence disproves, the (unfortunately very common) belief that the observed steeper descending phase of the cycle is **caused** by the rising trend. For electricity production, the rising trend has the precisely opposite effect.
[28] Goodwin 1950, 1951, 1953, 1955, 1967, 1972, 1982.

causation of trade cycles. This and more recent work along these lines, has been summarized and discussed critically by Krueger. [29]

The economic processes singled out by Goodwin are: [30]

> "... the very structure of capitalism constitutes a homeostatic mechanism which functions by means of variations in distributive shares but does so in such a way as to keep them constant in the long run. If real wages go up, profits go down; if profits go down, savings and investment lag, thus slowing up the creation of new jobs. But the labor force is continually growing both through natural increase and through men 'released' by technological progress. The reserve army of labor grows, wages lag behind the growth of productivity, profits rise, and accumulation is accelerated back to a high level. This in turn gradually reduces unemployment, wages rise, and so it goes on, indefinitely."

In spite of the impressive successes of models of this type, for instance in yielding a cycle of asymmetrical shape with a descent faster than the ascent, we wish to put forward the view that some **essential** elements of the puzzle have been omitted by models of this type. These elements are:

1. Investor confidence, or its converse, uncertainty of the future.
2. The distinction between what we may call "rentiers" and "entrepreneurs".

The models of Goodwin type fail to account for the sheer speed of the "crash" in the observed cycle. There is a decline, indeed, faster than the rise. However, this decline is smooth and regular. [31] In reality, the share market, in particular, reaches a rather sharp and narrow peak just before the onset of the crash, and then drops nearly vertically. The words "crash" and "panic", used by contemporaries, are by no means just poetic exaggerations. Goodwin type models, like most other trade cycle models, can not reproduce this behavior.

[29] Krueger 1982.

[30] Goodwin 1972 p.442.

[31] See Blatt 1983, p.209, for a typical numerical example.

In our view, this failure is not merely a question of an inappropriate choice of parameters within these models. The explanatory elements stressed by Goodwin are all very plausible and convincing at first sight. However, not one of them operates fast enough to explain the speed of the crash. The essential elements of these models, all of them related to the class struggle between capital and labor, are incapable of changing sufficiently rapidly in time:

1. Real wages do vary, but with nothing like the necessary speed.
2. To the extent that profits are merely an inverse reflection, so to speak, of real wage movements, profits must move equally slowly.
3. Natural increase in the labor force is regular, slow and even.
4. Technological progress may indeed go in sudden spurts, at the level of new inventions. However, we know only too well how long it takes before a new invention "penetrates" the economy, even today. This delay is very much larger in the nineteenth century, and thus the economic effects of technological progress (which is what matters for trade cycle theory) develop at a slow speed.

In our view, the failure of models of the Goodwin type to yield a sufficiently fast "crash" is inherent in the basic structure of these models, in their adherence to "real" economic factors, to the exclusion of all psychological factors.

As we stress throughout this book, psychological factors such as investor confidence can, and do frequently, change almost instantaneously, and a theory which includes such factors has no difficulty whatever in explaining the speed of the crash.

CHAPTER V: A First Look at the New Model

In this chapter we outline, in broad strokes, a schematic trade cycle model based on confidence and its fluctuations, and we support the basic points with evidence from economic history.

SECTION A: THE ACTORS.

There are three sectors (or groups of agents in the economy) interacting in our model:

1. Investors willing and able to place some of their wealth in shares and bonds of risky enterprises, in return for the promise of a future cash flow.
2. Company promoters and other entrepreneurs engaged in enterprises with significant amounts of time between commencement of the project and eventual financial returns. Many, but not all, of these projects involve the production of capital goods, such as railways and canals.
3. Everyone else.

In the Britain of the nineteenth century the comfortable and rich classes accumulated income so rapidly as to exceed all available possibilities of spending it on consumption, and to strain all modes of investment. [1] No doubt feudal and aristocratic societies would have succeeded in throwing away a great deal of this surplus in riotous living, luxury building, war and other uneconomic activities. A modern welfare society might attempt to distribute some of these vast accumulations for purposes of social amelioration. [2] In the nineteenth century neither course of action was even considered seriously.

Who was in this investor class? Jenks says: [3]

> "It was the country investor who was looking about most earnestly for reproductive investments. And by

---

[1] Jenks 1963 p.127 estimated the annual British surplus seeking investment at sixty million pounds in 1840.

[2] It would succeed, undoubtedly, in wasting much of the surplus on a topheavy and inefficient bureaucracy.

[3] Jenks 1963 p.72.

the 'country investor' is meant the totality of persons whose fortunes had been enhanced by the industrial changes of the preceding fifty years. These persons were by no means all engaged in manufacture or trade. Many had been so, but had purchased a country estate and were in a fair way to become swallowed up in the country families. Others, and those with large fortunes were of this sort, had been the fortunate proprietors of land upon which new factory towns sprang up or in which lucrative mining operations were carried on. High as their standards of consumption were, these magnates could not find use for the inflated rent rolls with which the Industrial Revolution had dowered them. It was from Lancashire, from Ireland, from the eastern and midland counties where the rent of land accumulated in sums which were not spent nor profitably invested locally that balances flowed constantly to the London bill-brokers."

Walter Bagehot remarks in "Lombard Street" that agricultural areas of Britain were normally creditors, and the industrial areas normally debtors in the London money market: [4]

"Commerce is curiously conservative in its homes, unless it is imperiously obliged to migrate. Partly from this cause, and partly from others, there are whole districts in England which cannot and do not employ their own money. No purely agricultural county does so. The savings of a country with good land but no manufactures and no trade much exceed what can be safely lent in the county. These savings are first lodged in the local banks, are by them sent to London, and are deposited with London bankers, or with bill brokers. In either case the result is the same. The money thus sent up from the accumulating districts is employed in discounting the bills of the industrial districts. Deposits are made with the bankers and bill brokers in Lombard Street by the bankers of such counties as Somersetshire and Hampshire, and those bill brokers and bankers employ them in the discount of bills from Yorkshire and Lancashire. Lombard Street is thus a perpetual agent between the two great divisions of England - between the rapidly-growing

[4] Bagehot 1873 p.6.

> districts, where almost any amount of money can be well and easily employed, and the stationary and the declining districts, where there is more money than can be used."

Thus, the investor class consists of landed gentry, and a few wealthy merchants. As they are not content to hoard their savings, they need to find profitable investments for them.

But where? Existing industries have become far too cheap to absorb more than a fraction of the surplus looking for investment: even supposing the size of the cotton industry to be doubled, the capital cost would absorb only a part of the available surplus. What is needed is a sponge large enough to take up the remainder of it.

This giant sponge is provided by the second group in our model, which consists of entrepreneurs engaged in risky enterprises such as the construction of railways. These are the people who issue shares and/or bonds to raise money. Although many, perhaps most, of the enterprises in question relate to the production of capital goods such as railways or canals, this is **not** the essential feature of our group 2. Rather, the essential feature consists of a significant **time lapse** between commencement of the project and the anticipated returns, a time lapse which makes any precise predictions impossible.

For example, the project of the South Sea Company around 1720 was not investment in conventional capital goods (it was the slave trade between Africa and America). Yet, the South Sea "bubble" remains, to this day, a prime example of a speculative project run by unscrupulous promoters using the public's money for their own benefit.

In neo-classical economic theory, the distinction between entrepreneurs and their investors is muted, to the point of almost complete disappearance. There exists a legal fiction that every investor holding shares in an enterprise is an active part-owner of that enterprise, with full knowledge of, and the ability to direct, its operations. This legal fiction is employed in neo-classical economics to eliminate the economic distinction between these two groups.

Yet, anyone reading an account of the goings-on in the nineteenth century, for example in connection with the construction of the railway network of the United States, [5]

[5] Josephson 1934.

is faced immediately by the incontrovertible fact that the entrepreneurs had interests and aims widely divergent from, and frequently directly opposed to, those of their investors.

An important consequence of this distinction arises when we look at the "incentive for real investment". By "real" investment we mean actual construction of railways, canals, or whatever; as opposed to "financial investment" in shares of these enterprises. [6]

In the conventional models of the trade cycle, the assumed causation is **from** changes in real output levels **to** the decision to commence real investment. This is the content of the well-known acceleration principle. [7] In an ideal world in which everything is done optimally, such a principle might well govern operations.

In the real world of the nineteenth century, however, this principle, if active at all, was overwhelmed completely by other effects. The "supply" of speculative enterprises in the nineteenth century may be considered infinitely elastic, or so close to it as not to signify. Some investment projects may have been excessively optimistic, some others were downright fraudulent; but there was never a shortage in the supply of projects, as such. The overriding "incentive for real investment" was, simply, the willingness of financial investors to place money into speculative projects. [8]

It is as important to realize what is omitted from a model, as what is included. Our third group, "everyone else", is treated purely schematically, via very rough assumptions coupled with some accounting identities. In our model, the driving force behind the trade cycle is the interaction between groups 1 and 2, and in particular the state of expectations and confidence of group 1. As long as confidence is high and rising, everything is fine. When confidence breaks and plunges, panic sets in.

---

[6] Called "placement" by Joan Robinson 1956 p.6.

[7] J.M. Clark 1917.

[8] On this view, the entrepreneurs played a rather less heroic role than postulated, for example, by Frank Knight (1921). The entrepreneurs in that period did not take major risks themselves, with their own money. Rather, they went around raising money from others, usually in England. If the project failed and the company went bankrupt, lots of people were bound to lose - but not our promoters.

Other economic groups, and their interactions, are surely of great importance for the economy as a whole:

1. Banks and other financial institutions should certainly be included in a more realistic model. In conditions of good trade, banks have considerable freedom of action and decision. However, if and when the banks' creditors lose confidence and start to withdraw their deposits, the banks are forced to contract their lending. The underlying cause of a crash is loss of confidence by the class of investors, not independent action by banks.
2. The interaction between labor and capital, stressed by so many economists, and so basic in Karl Marx's view, has much to tell us; yet labor is merely a part of "group 3" in our model. This point will be discussed further in chapter 9.

We maintain that, for the limited purpose of gaining an insight into the causation of the trade cycle, all other economic groups and their interactions are of less importance than groups 1 and 2.

SECTION B: THE PLOT.

Let us start our description of the trade cycle at a point near the beginning of the upswing phase. Confidence is low, having been shaken badly by a panic not so long ago. However, shares can be bought cheaply, and some shrewd investors decide that now is the time to buy.

This slows down and then reverses the collapse in share prices, but it takes some time before investor confidence has recovered enough so that new issues can be floated on the money market. Investors are at first interested only in shares of solid companies that have proved themselves by surviving the panic and the subsequent period of depression. It is not till later that our group 2, the entrepreneurs with new, risky, projects, are able to recommence their operations.

There now begins a cumulative process, the upward phase of the trade cycle. Share sales continue to improve. Share prices, having ceased to drop wildly, after a while commence an irregular, but generally upward, movement. As a result, after a while, more and more investors become willing, again, to place a fraction of their wealth into speculative enterprises, and this fraction itself tends to increase. Each passing month reinforces the fledgling confidence.

"Real" activity is stimulated by the resulting expenditures on speculative projects. Men are hired, raw materials are purchased, and the secondary effects of this soon pervade the whole economy. Furthermore, the gains made on the stock market are conceived by group 1 as being wealth in their hands, and their consumption of goods and services is boosted. Keynes stresses that stock exchange prices significantly affect consumption as the cycle progresses, particularly in the (later) downturn:

> "Unfortunately a serious fall in the marginal efficiency of capital also tends to affect adversely the propensity to consume. For it involves a severe decline in the market value of stock exchange equities. Now, on the class who take an active interest in their stock exchange investments, especially if they are employing borrowed funds, this naturally exerts a very depressing influence. These people are, perhaps, even more influenced in their readiness to spend by rises and falls in the value of their investments than by the state of their incomes. With a 'stock-minded' public as in the United States to-day, a rising stock market may be an almost essential condition of a satisfactory propensity to consume; and this circumstance, generally overlooked until lately, obviously serves to aggravate still further the depressing effect of a decline in the marginal efficiency of capital." [9]

Continuing our account, trade revives and continues to increase strongly. All the economic indicators look set for prosperity, thus reinforcing the rise of confidence in the money market.

Of course, as investors see an ever larger fraction of their total wealth tied up in shares, the rate at which they are prepared to, or able to, purchase new share issues levels off, though at a high level. We are now well into the "boom" phase.

Meanwhile, there are some ominous developments, not obvious to the investors.

---

[9] Keynes 1936 p.315.

The promoters have commenced their projects before having on hand all the funds to complete them. This seemed sensible both to them and to the more observant investors, as it should be in everybody's interest to finish the projects as soon as possible. The rest of the money would obviously (to them) be forthcoming later. As the flow of new funds levels off, however, this practice suddenly seems much less safe.

Economic growth theory tells us that a growing economy can support a rate of return equal to its rate of growth. [10] The average rate of growth in the nineteenth century was between two and four percent; this corresponds well to the rate of return offered on "risk-free" paper such as Consols. [11] Promoters of speculative projects had to offer significantly higher rates of return, so as to attract any funds at all. The actual rates offered started around ten percent, and went well up from there.

For example, describing the railway boom of the eighteen forties it was written that

> "So long as shares have a high premium ... with prospects of certain 10 per cent dividends ... interference was not contemplated." [12]

Note the words "certain 10 per cent" being offered. More examples, and quotes from contemporary sources can be found in Boyd (1986).

So much for the promises. Let us now turn to take a look at the performance.

As a rough guide to what was actually achieved as a return on capital by the kinds of investments we are here classifying as speculative, let us take statistics on railway revenues and costs for the year 1887-88, see Table 5.1. [13] Railway profits, especially in the U.S.A., were even smaller before then, since many of the regions served had little population or agriculture until after the coming of the railway.

For comparison, bank interest rates in 1887-88 were: London 3.3%, European average 3.7%. [14] Railway con-

---

[10] Von Neumann 1945; Kemeny 1956.

[11] Hawtrey 1938 (Appendix 1 p.281) lists the prices of 3 percent consols between 1844 and 1879.

[12] Evans 1848 p.13.

[13] Mulhall 1892 p.497.

[14] Mulhall 1892 p.640.

Table 5.1. RAILWAY CONSTRUCTION COSTS AND RETURNS (in pounds per rail mile).

	U.K.	U.S.A.	World
Construction costs	43600	12500	16100
Receipts per annum	3680	1290	1350
Running expenses	1910	900	830
Return on capital per annum	1770	390	520
Percentage on construction cost	4.1	3.1	3.2

struction returned little, if anything, more, in spite of involving the investor in high risk of total loss of his capital. Yet, despite these dismal realized profitability figures total railway mileages increased between 1880 and 1888 by 55.5% worldwide, by 66.6% in the U.S.A. [15] Indeed, mileage in Denmark increased by 47% despite a realized return of a pitiful 1.2%.

Thus our promoters are offering very much larger returns than they can really deliver. Note that it makes no difference to our argument whether a promoter is honest or dishonest. The honest promoter who is over-optimistic in his estimate of future returns, has exactly the same eventual effect as the crook out to fleece the suckers. The conservative promoter who offers no more than a realistic rate of return is crowded out of the money market by the bigger and better promises of his competitors for investment funds.

For some time the promoters have no difficulty in continuing to pay dividends on shares and interest on bonds. The laws, as interpreted by the judiciary at that time, permit such payments to be made out of subscriptions from new shareholders, and this is a common practice. [16]

However, as the rate of growth of the flow of new funds falls, some enterprises find themselves in difficulties and

[15] Mulhall 1892 p.495.

[16] Strictly speaking, the British Companies Clauses Act 1845, section 121 provided: "The company shall not make any dividend whereby their capital stock will be in any way reduced ... ". However, the Act then went on to permit this practice provided the company obtained the consent of all secured creditors. For details, see Gower 1969, chapters 2, 3, and 6.

are driven bankrupt. Their closures affect the confidence of the investing public. The loss of confidence is reinforced by further failures. Some investors initially, and then more and more of them, begin to question the wisdom of holding so much of their wealth in shares and bonds of speculative enterprises. Accordingly, they try to dispose of these pieces of paper.

At this point, they find to their horror that they can not! There are plenty of sellers, indeed, but mighty few buyers. A particular landed gentleman may dispose of his shares, to another landed gentleman with a more optimistic view of the future. The class of investors as a whole (our group 1) cannot decrease its total holding of shares.

The "panic" is now on, in earnest. Share values come tumbling down, in a matter of months or even weeks, from the heights they have reached in a seven- or eight-year period of rising confidence.

With no one willing to buy shares, the flow of wealth into speculative enterprises (group 2) comes to a complete halt. As a result, the cash position of those enterprises which have not already gone bankrupt changes from a steady deterioration to a violent and precipitous decline. More and more of them go bankrupt. These additional bankruptcies in turn depress confidence even further, daily reinforcing the feeling of hopelessness and despair. The "cumulative process" at work here is the reverse of the one occurring during the build-up of prosperity, except that it acts very much faster.

In its heedless, panic-stricken, downward rush, the money market is bound to go too far, to overcorrect. Shares of perfectly sound enterprises come tumbling down along with those in more rickety structures. Sooner or later, sensible and sober investors come to the conclusion that the money market is offering exceptionally good value for money.

And when that happens, we commence the next cycle.

In this chapter we have outlined the course of the historical trade cycle, according to the views of observers who have studied it closely, in a form which we shall proceed to express in equations as we build our mathematical model in subsequent chapters.

CHAPTER VI: **Confidence**

In the previous chapters we showed that a psychological variable representing investor confidence must be an essential element in a theoretical approach to the trade cycle. Before embarking on the construction of a schematic model of the cycle along these lines, a preliminary study of confidence, uncertainty and investment evaluation is essential.

A reasonably complete theory of these matters is in the literature. [1] We present a somewhat simplified version of that theory, sufficient for our purposes.

This, and later, chapters contain qualitative, non-mathematical explanations which serve as motivation for the mathematical equations of our model. These equations are collected together in Appendix C. At the end of every section, we shall list those equations for which that section has provided the qualitative justification. Non-mathematical readers may skip the equations without loss of continuity of the argument.

SECTION A: THE HORIZON OF UNCERTAINTY.

Consider an investor who has funds to place, in return for the promise of future dividends or interest payments. He is offered some investment project into which to put his money. Our investor wants to place a valuation on the investment offered, allowing for the effects of time and of uncertainty of return. How should he value the investment?

This question is an old one, and the conventional answer is in terms of discounted present value of the future cash flow. Take a constant future cash flow of x dollars per year, for simplicity. If the discount rate is taken to be r (equivalent to 100r percent per year), then the present value of such a cash flow is equal to x/r. [2]

If the cash flow is completely riskless, then the appropriate discount rate is the standard rate of return on riskless investments, for example on government bonds (consols in nineteenth century Britain). We shall denote this rate by the symbol r0.

---

[1] Blatt 1983 chapters 12 and 13.

[2] Brealey 1981 pp.10-30.

However, we are not concerned with those investors who placed their money in consols. We wish to obtain a valuation of speculative enterprises, where uncertainty is an important factor. A landed gentleman who invests in American railroads or in Australian gold fields can not possibly be completely unaware of the uncertainty attaching to such investments.

To allow for the basic principle that "A safe dollar is worth more than a risky one", the appropriate discount rate is conventionally adjusted by adding a "risk premium", which we shall call r*, to the risk free rate of return. [3] Empirically the risk premium was, and still is, extremely significant. In the nineteenth century, the risk-free rate r0 was around 2 to 4 percent. Risky investments, on the other hand, offered around ten percent or more even in good times, and a great deal more when investors were reluctant. [4] Thus, if we write $r = r0 + (r - r0) = r0 + r^*$, then the second part (the risk premium r*) was by far the larger contribution to r.

Neo-classical theory is strangely silent on what determines the size of the risk premium r*. The main thrust of this theory requires a supposedly purely rational calculation of possibilities in a future which is either assumed to be known with certainty or (at worst) for which subjective probabilities of all possible outcomes are assigned by the investor and are taken seriously by him.

J.E. Meade presents the neo-classical theory of risk, and states its limitations clearly:

> "We have so far spoken of this process of choice by Mr A of policies in conditions of risk and uncertainty as if he had a clear idea of what was the probability which he should attach to each possible outcome which might result from each policy ... This type of chance approximates to a straightforward gamble on throwing dice, tossing coins, playing roulette, and so on. Cases of this kind we may call cases of risk rather than uncertainty. ... At the other extreme is the sort of case in which there does not exist that past experience of large numbers of similar past cases on which to base an estimate of the chances. Such a case might arise with the invention of a new product." [5]

[3] Brealey 1981, see especially the graph on page 50.
[4] See the discussion in chapter 5, also see Boyd (1986).

Nineteenth century investors were almost always in the latter category:

1. The nineteenth century investor was placing money into projects which did not go into production for many years, such as a railway or a canal. Therefore he could build up no set of probabilities of an eventual profit based on experience.
2. The promoters of the project did not inform the investor of details of how the company was faring. On the contrary, the promoters took great pains to make it appear as if the project were going well.

This sort of theory can indeed tell us, that as time goes on and the investors see very few failures, experience tells them that the probability of failure is very small - until "their" company crashes and they are forced to change their minds.

It is the essence of speculative investments that the future is not known with certainty, or indeed known at all. Alternatives in the future can not be assigned meaningful probabilities. We are convinced that the concept of "probability" must not be used in the context of unique events such as bankruptcies of major concerns. Such a "probability" is not merely of unknown numerical value - it does not even have an unambiguous definition.

Intuitively we all know that a psychological factor, which we may call "confidence in the future", matters very much for the risk premium r*. Let us see whether we can make this relationship a bit more explicit.

It makes a great deal of difference how far we are looking into the future. The near future is much less uncertain than the more distant future. In the near future we feel that we can make reasonable guesses as to what may happen, and assign subjective probabilities to the alternatives. The most likely eventuality is that things will continue pretty much as they are now. This outcome becomes very much less likely if we attempt to look farther ahead.

The simplest way to approach the "risk premium" is by (provisionally) ignoring the risk-free rate of return r0 altogether, so that the entire rate r is a rate of return for risk. Let us introduce a symbol for the reciprocal of r,

---

[5] Meade 1968 pp.437-438.

namely the letter f. Then the conventional valuation formula $V = x/r$ takes the equivalent form: $V = fx$.

r is a discount rate, a fraction per unit of time (per year). Thus its reciprocal $f = 1/r$ has the dimension of a time. We shall think of f as a "horizon of uncertainty", and we interpret the valuation formula $V = fx$ as follows: If the risk-free rate of return is zero, then the valuation V is obtained by multiplying the yearly cash flow x by the number of years f that we are prepared to trust our predictions of the future, that is, by the number of years before uncertainty closes in to the point that all predictions become meaningless. [6]

More precisely our "horizon of uncertainty" is the reciprocal of the risk premium only, i.e., $f = 1/r^*$. We shall ignore this refinement in what follows. The risk-free rate of return $r0$ is one of the many, less essential, factors omitted from our cut-down model.

Thus, "investor confidence" can be described by a psychological variable f which has the dimension of time, and has the intuitive meaning of a "horizon of uncertainty", a time beyond which the investor does not believe the future course of events to be predictable.

Clearly, f increases as "confidence" increases, and decreases when there are shocks to confidence. It is said that at the time of the Communist Chinese victory in mainland China, in 1948, investment confidence in the British Crown Colony of Hong Kong was so low that no risky project could be launched if its financial success needed more than half a year of operation in the future. When it became clear, some time later, that the new Communist government in China had no intention of attacking Hong Kong, investment confidence revived, and the horizon of uncertainty f increased again to more normal values.

---

[6] This interpretation assumes positive cash flow x for a time f, no cash flow after that. Strictly speaking, in a more rigorous theory, the purchaser of shares in a nineteenth century company could be faced with a negative cash flow after the company failed, and thus lose more than he invested. This possibility is dealt with in the more mathematical discussion, see Blatt (1983), but will be ignored here. For further discussion, see Boyd (1986).

SECTION B: INCREASING AND DECREASING CONFIDENCE.

Once we recognize that the "risk premium" r* is basically a psychological variable, and that it is easier to work with its reciprocal f, we can proceed to make some rough guesses about how this quantity f may change in time. Suppose we are in the upswing period of the trade cycle, with no violent shocks to confidence. Then we should expect confidence to increase more or less steadily as time goes on. As the time since the last "panic" increases, the memory of that panic becomes less vivid, and investors become more willing to look farther into the future with confidence that their predictions and expectations will be met. [7]

Thus, in the absence of shocks to confidence, we shall assume that f increases steadily. The precise rate of increase is unknown, and its value is not of crucial importance for our theory. Within our model, we make the simplest possible assumption, which is that f increases (other things being equal) by one year for every year that has elapsed.

What makes confidence decrease? At first glance, one might think that the true position of the project, its current balance sheet and cash flow position, should be the dominant factor. However, investors in the nineteenth century were rarely provided with this information, and many of them were in no position to read such financial statements critically. A landed gentleman in some sleepy hamlet of East Anglia might have money placed in U.S. railways, but it is unlikely that he had even the vaguest idea of the true financial status of "his" railway. Certainly, the entrepreneurs in the U.S.A. who controlled the railway company were not at all eager to help our investor to a realistic appreciation of the state of his investment.

Things changed suddenly, however, when the railway company was declared **bankrupt**. At one stroke, the bonds and shares of this company became just so much expensive wallpaper. The landed gentlemen who had invested money had lost it all, and investors in other companies had their confidence in the future shaken badly. Throughout the nine-

[7] Note that this steady increase of confidence runs counter to the factual situation. Actually, as time goes on, we are coming closer to the next crash. However, typical investors then, and probably still today, do not react in this cold, logical fashion.

teenth century, "panics" were initiated by some spectacular bankruptcy or other. A company in financial trouble could, and did, conceal its problems from its investors as long as possible. But it is impossible to conceal bankruptcy.

In our model, therefore, the time development of the confidence variable f is based on two terms: (1) A positive constant term which makes f increase steadily in the absence of shocks to confidence, and (2) A negative term which is an increasing function of the "bankruptcy rate", B, of speculative enterprises.

This bankruptcy rate is defined as follows: Consider a short time interval dt. During this time interval, a fraction Bdt of all speculative enterprises are declared bankrupt. Thus, if B is equal to a steady 0.02, say, then two percent (by value) of all speculative enterprises declare bankruptcy during a full year. [8] When B rises, f starts to go down, at a rate increasing with B.

Clearly, such purely schematic, simplistic assumptions should be out of place in an econometric model. However, our model is not intended for detailed data fitting, but to elucidate the underlying causal mechanism of the trade cycle. For this purpose, and for this purpose only, we are permitted to use extremely rough, skeletal assumptions; and this is what we do.

The considerations of sections A and B are embodied in the model equation C.1 [9] (meaning: equation 1 of Appendix C) for the model variable f, the horizon of confidence. a1 is a constant parameter; numerical values of all parameters are listed in Appendix C. We shall use the symbol "*" to mean a multiplication sign. The equation reads:

(C.1) df/dt = 1 - a1*B*f

[8] In our theory, B shows some very rapid variations, particularly during the downswing of the trade cycle; thus B is not expected to remain constant for years on end; the example just given is intended purely to illustrate the meaning of the variable B.

[9] We remind the non-mathematical reader that study of this, and later, equations is not required for understanding the material which follows.

SECTION C: THE MONEY MARKET.

Stock markets and share issues existed on a large scale throughout the nineteenth century, starting with the canal companies: "Canal shares became freely negotiable and were quoted on the Stock Exchange like government securities at the end of the eighteenth century." [10] Public utilities, insurance companies and even one brewery were quoted on the exchange after 1809.

Hyndman [11] gives figures on the number and value of new share issues on the London Stock Exchange during the boom prior to the crisis of 1825. The total amounted to 114 companies, with a gross capital of upwards of one hundred million pounds sterling.

The 1830's and 1840's brought a flood of railway shares to the exchange, although manufacturing businesses were mostly not quoted until after 1850. [12]

Let us now adapt our simplified investment evaluation theory to develop a, very crude, equation for the movement of share market prices. Consider a share whose current market price is P and which is paying a dividend yield on that price of j (that is, the share pays dividends of $x = jP$ per annum). Then, if the share is bought and held, our evaluation formula gives a subjective valuation of $V = fx = fjP$.

This valuation, assuming the variables within to be constantly changing, and the market to take time to adjust, will rarely equal the current price P of the share. Now, the investor in negotiable securities needs to predict short term price movements. If his valuation of the share is above the market price he will buy, hoping to reap a real gain from the impending adjustment of the market to the 'fundamental worth' of the share. If his valuation is significantly below the market price, he will not buy and will try to dispose of any shares he is holding currently. Thus if V exceeds P, investors will tend to bid up the share price. Conversely if V falls below P, investors will attempt to sell and this tends to depress the price. Therefore the factor indicating the direction of share price movements in the immediate future is the difference $V-P = fjP-P = (fj-1)P$. The market mechanism, which we have described, is continually adjusting the price P of the share

[10] Mathias 1969 p.117.
[11] Hyndman 1892 pp.28-29.
[12] Mathias 1969 p.384.

towards the valuation V=fjP, trying to bring this difference to zero, but with a significant time delay.

From now on, the symbol P will be used, not for the actual price of any one particular share, but for a **general index of share prices.** We shall let P = 1 stand for the share price index at the beginning of the upswing phase of the trade cycle, so that P > 1 indicates buoyant share market conditions, and P < 1 indicates a low, depressed share market.

Let us use the symbol D for the **fractional rate of change of the share price index P,** that is D = (1/P)(dP/dt) = (d/dt)(log P). From the argument just given, it is plausible to include within D a term proportional to the non-dimensional quantity: fj-1. The constant of proportionality, which we shall call b, has the dimension of 1/time. The larger the value of b, the quicker is the adaptation of share prices to a change in subjective valuation.

In the model, there are a number of such constants b, each denoting a rate of adaptation of actual to desired or intended or predicted values. In an econometric model, each b has to be estimated separately from the data. In our purely schematic model, however, we use the extreme simplification of just two values of b: A value b1 = 1 for the rate of adaptation of "financial" quantities, and a second, slower rate b2 = 0.3 for "real" investment activities. These correspond to adjustment times of one year, and a bit more than three years, respectively.

The subjective long-term valuation of future cash flows is one main factor in influencing share price movements. A second factor which must be taken into account is the **immediate** effect of a high rate of bankruptcies on the motion of share prices. There can be no doubt that the money market reacts immediately, and very strongly, to the announcement of one or more major bankruptcies. Thus, the rate of change D is influenced directly and immediately by a high bankruptcy rate, not merely indirectly via f. We have included a negative term in the mathematical equation for D, equal to -a3*B where B is the bankruptcy rate and a3 is a dimensionless constant parameter equal to 2 in our simulations.

A third term in D arises from factors which tend to arrest the fall of P before share prices drop all the way to zero. As the market tumbles down in a panic, there are bound to be some sharp and sober investors, as well as some optimistic fools, who feel that the drop has gone far enough, that prices have come down to unreasonably low levels and are bound to recover soon. Particular investors are likely to differ in their judgment of the correct time to enter the market as buyers, so that there is no hard and fast "lower barrier" to the share price index P. But there is a "soft barrier". As P drops lower and lower, increasing numbers of potential buyers decide that the time to buy has arrived. Thus, the very fall of share prices sets in motion forces tending to arrest that fall.

In our schematic model, the soft barrier effect starts when P drops below P1 = 0.8, and the effect increases the farther P drops below P1. There is no particular merit in the precise figure 0.8, but the precise value is not of major qualitative importance for the results.

The considerations of this section are embodied in the model equations C.9 for D, and C.10 for P. In these equations, "b1", "b4", "a3", "P1" and "j" are constants, i.e., model parameters. For "u1" see section D. For the function ramp(x), see equation C.4.

(C.9) $\dot{D}$ = b1*(fj - 1) - a3*B + (b4/P)*ramp(P1 - P) + u1

(C.10) dP/dt = PD

SECTION D: RANDOM EFFECTS.

It would be a rash person indeed who claims that he can predict share price movements in detail and with mathematical precision. Whatever may be the systematic causes of share price variations, there also exist all sorts of unpredictable influences, sudden rumors, without visible source but with very visible effects, unexpected news, good or bad, sudden shifts from unfounded optimism to equally unfounded pessimism and vice versa; the thousand and one causes of variations in "market sentiment" which are utterly beyond hope of mathematical prediction.

Thus, after the most important causes of systematic variations have been allowed for, it is still necessary to include "random shocks" of the sort always assumed by econometricians. In most of the equations of our model, we have dispensed with random shock terms, on the grounds that these terms, though likely to be present, have only minor effects on the course of the trade cycle. But for share price variations (and for the bankruptcy rate B as well) random shock terms should be included. Share prices do not move in a simple, regular, straight line fashion. They fluctuate up and down like the proverbial "random walk". [13] We have introduced a random shock term into equation C.9 for D in order to reproduce this type of behavior (the term "u1").

However, we differ from Samuelson in allowing for systematic, longer-term, cyclical variations of share prices apart from, and on top of, these "random walk" variations. Indeed, the basic trend of the trade cycle is unrelated to the random walk effect, but is related closely to the systematic effects.

If the random shocks are omitted from the model, the movements of the share market are too systematic, too regular, too even - but they still reproduce the main and essential features of the trade cycle. By contrast, if the systematic effects are omitted, and all the emphasis is placed on the random effects, then the resulting "cycle" bears only a superficial resemblance to what happens in reality, as we saw in chapter 4.

To support our critical view of the random walk model of the stock market, let us quote from Granger and Morgenstern who have studied actual twentieth century stock markets. By using spectral analysis they conclude: [14]

> "The evidence from the spectra therefore clearly suggests that although the random walk hypothesis is extremely successful in explaining most of the spectral shape it does not adequately explain the strong long run (24 months or more) components of the series."

These "long run components" are on a time scale comparable to a cycle. We interpret them as cyclical phenomena which are not explained properly by the pure random walk model.

The considerations of section D are embodied in the term "u1" of model equation C.9 for D, as well as in equation C.20 for the random variable u1. In this equation, rt12 is the square root of 12, and r1 is a random variable uniformly distributed in the interval (0,1). b5 is a constant.

(C.20) u1 = rt12*b5*(r1 - 0.5)

[13] Samuelson 1965a, 1965b.
[14] Granger 1970 p.141.

CHAPTER VII: Description of the Model

In this chapter we will complete the description of our model, and exhibit some typical simulations. This model represents our view of the essential causation of the business cycle.

We have introduced the actors, and outlined the plot of our story, in chapter 5; we have discussed confidence and the money market in chapter 6. Let us now motivate the rest of the new model.

The mathematical equations are collected together in Appendix C; there also can be found numerical values for the parameters used for our simulations. At the end of each section of this chapter, we list those equations for which that section has provided the discussion and qualitative justification.

SECTION A: PRICES.

We take the price level of everything **except shares** to be simply constant: P = 1 for the price index. Thus there is no distinction, in the model, between real and nominal quantities, except (most important) for the money market.

Clearly, all types of price variations occurred in reality, but equally clearly, the price level of shares was much more volatile than either the money wage or the real wage. Thus, it is not prima facie inconsistent to ignore commodity price and wage variations and retain money market variations; but one should have to think of very special arguments to justify the opposite neglect. [1]

In any case, however, our model's neglect of most (but not all) price variations is well in line with conventional practice in this area of theoretical economics. We call attention to the fact that **most** of the standard models of the trade cycle work exclusively with "real" quantities, with no attention whatever to price variations.

---

[1] This is the point at which our model differs fundamentally from trade cycle models of the Goodwin type, see section 4D.

SECTION B: THE DESIRED INVESTMENT FRACTION.

In addition to the valuation of financial investments, we must pay attention to the fraction of their total perceived wealth that our group 1, the investors, desire to hold in the form of shares and bonds. We shall denote this fraction by the symbol G and refer to it as the "desired investment fraction".

Clearly, this fraction can not be negative, nor (in the absence of an explicit banking sector) can it be larger than unity. When share prices are rising, G is likely to increase also; but not indefinitely, since G can not exceed unity. When share prices are falling, G will have a tendency to decrease; but again not indefinitely so.

In our model, we assume that the rate of change of G with time is proportional to the fractional rate of change of share prices, D. That is, the faster share prices rise, the faster (ceteris paribus) does the desired investment fraction G rise as well. However, the proportionality factor in this proportion depends both on the present value of G and on whether share prices are moving up or down at the moment. The reasoning underlying this assumption runs as follows:

An investor who already holds a major fraction of his perceived wealth in the form of shares is likely to become a bit slower in purchasing further shares, in consequence. Thus, in our model, G continues rising as long as D remains positive, but the **rate** of this rise slows down as G comes closer to 1. For simplicity, the rate of rise dG/dt contains a plain factor 1-G for this case, a factor which approaches zero as G approaches one. This slows down the rate of rise of G when G gets close to unity, and prevents G from rising above unity.

We can not leave it at this, however. The same effect which slows down the desire to buy in a situation where share prices are rising but G is already sizeable, does not slow down the desire to sell when share prices are dropping. On the contrary, the desire to sell, and sell quickly, is then increased. Thus, the factor 1-G gives a wrong result when D is negative. We get qualitatively correct results by making the factor of proportionality depend on the sign of D, as follows: 1-G for rising prices (D positive), and 1+G for falling prices (D negative).

We make no claim whatever that these rough and ready assumptions are correct quantitatively; but we believe that they do reproduce an important qualitative feature of the psychology of investors in the money market.

After these modifications, G can no longer rise above unity, and behaves in a qualitatively correct fashion when G is near unity. G could, however, still fall through zero and become negative, which is also an impossibility. To avoid this, we modify the equation for the time development of G when G becomes equal to zero. [2] In this eventuality (G = 0), we use the ordinary formula for dG/dt if and only if dG/dt is positive (in which case G can not go negative at this moment); however, if G is zero and at the same time the computed value of dG/dt is negative (so that G is about to go negative), the time derivative dG/dt is set equal to zero so that G remains equal to zero during the next time interval.

This procedure sounds extremely artificial; and so it is. However, this does not signify, for the following reason: When G is zero, or close to zero, we are near the bottom of a crash. The investors do not wish to invest anything, on the contrary, they wish to divest themselves of all shares in their possession. The precise mathematical behavior of G or of dG/dt in such a situation has no economic significance whatever. All that matters is that no one wishes to invest money in shares.

The considerations of this section are embodied in the differential equation C.2 for G, with the auxiliary, defining equations C.3 and C.4. a2, b3 and G1 are model parameters.

(C.2) $$dG/dt = a2*[1 - G*\mathrm{sign}(D)]*D + b(G)$$

(C.3) $$b(G) = (b3/G)*\mathrm{ramp}(G1 - G)$$

(C.4) $$\mathrm{ramp}(x) = \begin{cases} x & \text{if } x >= 0, \\ 0 & \text{if } x < 0. \end{cases}$$

[2] For purely numerical, computer reasons, the actual lower barrier used is not at G = 0, but rather at a slightly positive value, G1 = 0.01, and the barrier is "soft" rather than "hard" (see equations C.2 and C.3). However, this is merely a technical detail, unlike the soft barrier for the share price index P, which has economic meaning and significance.

SECTION C: FINANCIAL INVESTMENT AND CONSUMPTION.

Closely allied to the desired investment fraction G is the actual flow of investment funds, from our group 1 to speculative entrepreneurs (group 2). We shall use the symbol L for the flow rate of this financial investment, and the symbol A1 for the **perceived** asset position of the investors. By "perceived" we mean that the market valuation of their shares and bonds is counted as part of their assets.

The "desired" financial investment is the desired investment fraction G, multiplied by the total perceived assets A1. The actual financial investment [3] is the value J of outstanding shares and bonds. If the desired and actual values agree, there is (on the average) no incentive to place more money into shares. But if the desired value exceeds the actual value, the difference G*A1-J is available for placement, and will be placed at some rate; as usual, the rate constant b for this adjustment process is assigned the common value b1=1 for all "financial" adjustment rates.

Furthermore, there is an important asymmetry here. When desired investment exceeds actual investment, newly issued shares and bonds are bought and cash flows towards speculative enterprises. But when desired investment is **less** than actual investment, there is no corresponding cash flow backwards from speculative enterprises to investors.

Financial investment in our model (and in the real world of the nineteenth century) is irreversible. Some particular landed gentleman or wealthy merchant can sell his shares to some other member of the investing class, indeed. But the **class** of investors can no more rid itself of excess shares, than the community as a whole can rid itself of excess paper money in an inflation.

For this reason, the equation which determines the flow rate L of financial investments (equation C.8) is "one-sided". L can never be negative.

Next, we need to say something about consumption expenditure by our group 1. Consumption is taken to depend upon perceived income flow y of this group, where "perceived" means that our wealthy gentlemen count capital gains in the

---

[3] At this point, our model is (knowingly) ignoring the distinction between face value and market value of these investments. A more elaborate model should have two separate quantities J, one being the face value, the other the market value.

share market as "income", as foreshadowed in the previous chapter. [4] In equation C.5 for y, the first term v' is an (assumed constant) rental income (mainly for land), j is an (assumed constant) dividend rate, the term jJ is the flow of dividend income, DJ is the rate of capital gain (if D is positive) of the share portfolio of group 1, -BJ is the rate of capital loss due to bankruptcies. The term "q" is zero for now; it will be discussed in chapter 8.

Desired consumption c* of group 1 is an increasing function of perceived income y as long as y is positive, and is taken to be zero otherwise. (Note that y can and does go negative during a crash, as a result of rapid downward valuation of shares and a high rate of bankruptcies at the height of the panic.) For large positive y, the formula we use for c* is constructed in such a way that c* saturates (at a high level), so that the marginal propensity to consume is variable. In the simulations shown in section G, this marginal propensity equals 0.75 when perceived income y equals the land rent v'. It exceeds 0.75 when y < v'. The marginal propensity for desired consumption decreases with increasing perceived income y, eventually approaching zero as y becomes exceedingly large.

Actual consumption c of group 1 is determined by a "financial" adjustment process, with b1 = 1 as usual.

The considerations of this section are embodied in equations: C.5 for y, C.6 for c*, C.7 for dc/dt, and C.8 for L. Furthermore, there are two related accounting identities: equation C.11 for the rate of change of the perceived total assets A1 of group 1, and equation C.12 for their total current investment in shares, J.

(C.5) $y = v' + (D + j - B)*J + q$

(C.6) $c* = k'*\text{ramp}[y/(y + k'')]$

(C.7) $dc/dt = b1*(c* - c)$

[4] This is another rough-and-ready assumption. Clearly, at least some wealthy gentlemen must have been a bit more cautious than that. Thus, the perceived income should include some, but not all, of the capital gains on the share market. For our purposes, the very rough assumption of "all" is clearly closer to the truth than its opposite, "none"; and it has to be one or the other for such a schematic model.

(C.8) L = b1*A1*ramp[G - (J/A1)]

(C.11) d(A1)/dt = y - c

(C.12) dJ/dt = L + (D - B)J

SECTION D: THE BANKRUPTCY RATE.

We use a very rough-and-ready method to arrive at a crude approximation to the rate of bankruptcy B. Let us use the symbol A2 for the **cash** position of our second group.

A modern accountant may wish to include among the company assets the "book value" of, let us say, a half-completed railroad. For our purposes, this should be inappropriate. When bankruptcy looms ahead, when panic reigns in the market place and the creditors are demanding their money with threats and menaces, this book value is a largely imaginary quantity. Even if there are buyers willing to take over the incomplete project, these buyers have no intention of paying whatever the project has cost so far (which is the usual book value). On the contrary, the buyers, if there are any, are out to pay as little as they can get away with. Thus, accounting conventions which may be entirely valid in normal times, must not be applied in a panic. This explains why we concentrate on the **cash** position A2 of our second group.

This A2 is a consolidated account, for group 2 as a whole. When we look at individual companies or projects, their cash positions are bound to show a distribution of some kind, with some being better off than the average, others being worse off. The companies "at risk" are the ones in the "lower tail" of this distribution, with cash positions at or below zero. The "area under the tail" is a measure of the proportion of all companies at immediate risk of bankruptcy. [5]

---

[5] There exist neo-classical formulas for investment valuation under uncertainty, which make the valuation depend upon the distribution of expected outcomes. However, most of these formulas are based on the mean and the variance of this distribution. The variance is a measure of the "width of the peak", whereas our approach concentrates on the "area under the lower tail". For a general, largely unknown, dis-

As a very crude first guess, we pretend that this entire distribution moves, to the right or to the left, as a whole, with each individual company keeping its relative position within the distribution. On this basis, the "area under the tail" increases if and only if the consolidated cash position (the value of A2) worsens, i.e., if and only if A2 has a negative rate of change with time. When this happens, the rate at which companies enter the danger region for bankruptcy, is proportional to -d(A2)/dt, and the factor of proportionality is a function of A2, a function which increases as the consolidated cash position A2 worsens; for as this happens, the value of the density function of the distribution at the danger point (at zero) increases so that a given negative time rate of change d(A2)/dt brings ever more companies into the danger region. In the mathematical model, we have taken the factor of proportionality to be 1/A2. We hold no special brief for this simple assumption; other inverse dependences could be used equally well.

One should also include, in any formula for the rate of bankruptcies, a "random shock" element; otherwise the results are unrealistically regular and systematic. We do include such random shocks in our formula, in general; though in some of our simulations we ignore them for the sake of simplicity. The shocks make the results less regular and repetitive, so that successive cycles no longer resemble each other as closely as they do without these shocks. However, the shocks do not have any major qualitative effects on the course of the trade cycle in our model.

We are aware of the inadequacies of this crude, schematic model. For example, our mathematical formula for B implies (in the absence of random shocks) that no one at all goes bankrupt as long as the consolidated cash position of group 2 is improving, a patent absurdity. However, there are two reasons not to worry excessively about this shortcoming:

1. Small values of the bankruptcy rate (such as one might expect under conditions of "good trade") make rather little difference within our model. The bankruptcy rate B plays an important role if and only if it assumes big values. Exactly under these circumstances, the very crude, rough approximation on which our equation is based should not cause any qualitative trouble (though

---

tribution of possible outcomes, there exists no clear quantitative relationship between these two measures.

one should hardly expect to be able to use it for quantitative, econometric work).
2. The "random shock" term implies that B occasionally takes on non-zero values even when A2 is currently increasing with time.

The results of this section are embodied in equations: C.13 for B, and C.21 for the random shock term u2 within B.

(C.13) B = ramp[-(1/A2)(d(A2)/dt)+ u2]

(C.21) u2 = rt12*b6*(r2 - 0.5)

SECTION E: FLOW OF FUNDS AND ACTIVITY OF ENTREPRENEURS.

We denote the rate of real investment expenditure on speculative projects by the symbol z. In our simple model, the activity of speculative entrepreneurs is correlated directly with the flow of funds coming forth for such projects. However, the correlation can not be instantaneous. By definition, these are projects with long "latency times", for example, construction of a railroad. Time is needed to plan, to obtain the necessary labor and raw materials; none of which can be done to any great extent until after the entrepreneur has managed to raise a considerable sum of money, enough to see the project through its initial stages.

Thus, the activity level z at time t (measured in value terms) is governed by an adjustment equation to a "desired" level z*; the time constant b in that adjustment equation is taken to be b2=0.3. This adjustment rate corresponds to an adjustment time of a bit over three years for "real" (as opposed to "financial") investment activities. [6]

The "desired" activity level z* is governed primarily by financial considerations. z* is taken to be proportional to

[6] In a more elaborate model, it is desirable to describe this adjustment by a process of higher order, so as to capture, within the model, the slow rise of project expenditures in the initial years. Although this change would produce better simulations, we have refrained from introducing it into our schematic model.

the rate of flow of funds from investors, which we have denoted by L before. The constant of proportionality ($a5$ in equation C.16) is taken to be larger than unity, for the following reason: In the nineteenth century, it was common practice for entrepreneurs in our group 2 to commence activity on their projects well before they had gathered all the funds for full completion of the project. [7] If the constant of proportionality is merely equal to one, then this feature of the true situation is not reproduced adequately. We have taken the constant of proportionality to be 2; we consider this value to be rather conservative. The precise value of this constant is of only minor consequence for our results.

In addition to this intentional adjustment process for entrepreneurial activity, there is another, involuntary process caused by bankruptcies. When a company is declared bankrupt, all activity on its projects ceases. For this reason, we have included, within the equation governing the behavior of z (equation C.17), a negative term equal to the product of the bankruptcy rate B and the activity level z.

Let us now look at the overall flow of funds for the entrepreneurial group. There are a number of terms in this:

1. Entrepreneurs receive investment funds from group 1 at the flow rate L.
2. Entrepreneurs pay out dividends at the flow rate $j*J$ where J is the value [8] of outstanding shares and j is the promised rate of return. We take j to be simply a constant, equal to 0.12 (12 percent) in the simulations shown in section G.
3. Entrepreneurs expend funds at the activity rate z.
4. Finally, entrepreneurs receive a "rental for the use of capital goods" from our group 3, "everyone else". This third group is treated purely schematically. We assume that a certain fraction (1/4) of their receipts from

[7] For example the railroad builders in the boom leading up to the crash of 1873 had to stop building partway through construction because of an inability to sell additional securities to obtain the rest of the money needed to finish the line (see section 2C).

[8] Here is another point at which one should really make a distinction between the face value and the market value of shares; but we do without this refinement.

sales to groups 1 and 2, go back to group 2 as rental for capital.

Based on this flow of funds, there is then an accounting identity (equation C.15) for the current cash position A2 of our group 2; this cash position, in turn, enters into their rate of bankruptcy B.

The results of this section are embodied in equations: C.14 for the capital rental v", C.15 for the time derivative of A2 (this is an accounting identity), C.16 for the desired activity level z*, and C.17 for the realized activity level z.

(C.14) $v'' = a4*(c + z)$

(C.15) $d(A2)/dt = v'' + L - z - jJ$

(C.16) $z* = a5*L$

(C.17) $dz/dt = b2*(z* - z) - Bz$

SECTION F: GROUP 3.

Our third group, "everyone else", is treated purely schematically, via very rough assumptions coupled with an accounting identity.

The flow of external sales revenue to group 3 (we assume that all transactions internal to group 3 are proportional to external sales) consists of two terms:

1. Sales of (luxury) consumption goods to our group 1, the investors, at a flow rate c.
2. Sales of raw materials and/or labor services to group 2, in accordance with their activity level z.

Set off against these inflows there are two sources of outflow of funds:

1. Rental for the use of land (mainly in agriculture), paid to the landed gentry (group 1), together with a part of profits on traditional merchant activities such as textiles, paid to the wealthy merchants in group 1. We take this to be a constant term, for the reason that

rental contracts in the nineteenth century were fairly long-term (ten to twenty years) and therefore rentals could not change significantly on the time scale of the trade cycle, particularly not over the time span of a typical crash.

2. Rental for the use of capital goods, paid to the entrepreneurs in group 2; this is given by equation (C.14) in our model.

Putting together all four of these terms, we get an accounting balance equation (equation C.18) for the asset position A3 of our third group. This variable A3 does not react back on anything else in our model, but it is of interest to check that A3 does not turn negative, or become unreasonably large, as we go through a number of cycles.

$$(C.18) \quad d(A3)/dt = c + z - v' - v''$$

In summary, the model has nine endogenous variables: A1, A2, A3, c, f, G, J, P, and z. Their behavior is governed by nine differential equations: C.1, C.2, C.7, C.10, C.11, C.12, C.15, C.17, and C.18. The only exogenous variables (so far) are the time t and the random shock terms u1 and u2 (equations C.20 and C.21). We shall introduce one further exogenous variable, q, in chapter 8. All other symbols represent either (1) model parameters (constants), or (2) "auxiliary" quantities computable directly from the nine endogenous variables. These auxiliary quantities are: B, c*, D, L, v", y, z*. They are defined by equations: C.5, C.6, C.8, C.9, C.13, C.14, and C.16.

SECTION G: SIMULATIONS OF THE MODEL.

Having described the assumptions underlying our model, let us now see what results follow from the model equations. The simulation results plotted in figures 7.1 to 7.4 show the typical behavior of a number of the interesting variables of our model. Figure 7.1 contains the confidence variable f, the share price index P, and the cash flow L to entrepreneurs plotted on the same time scale, for a forty-year period covering approximately four complete cycles. The advantage of plotting several variables on the same figure is that the timing relationships become easier to see. Figure 7.2 contains the desired investment fraction G, the

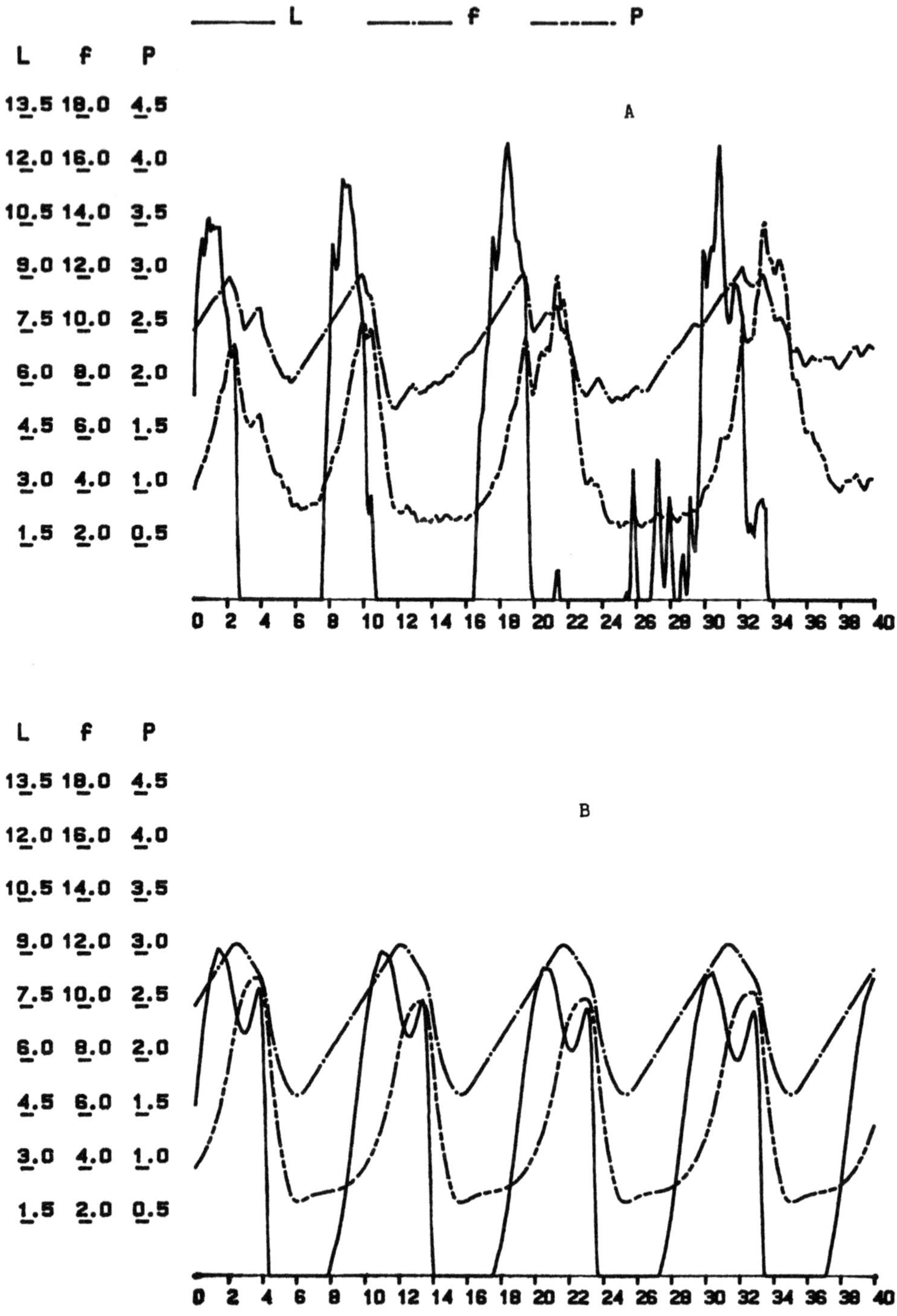

Fig. 7.1. A (top) Stochastic, B (bottom) deterministic simulation. Confidence f (years), share price index P, flow of funds to group 2 (million pounds/annum); vs. time.

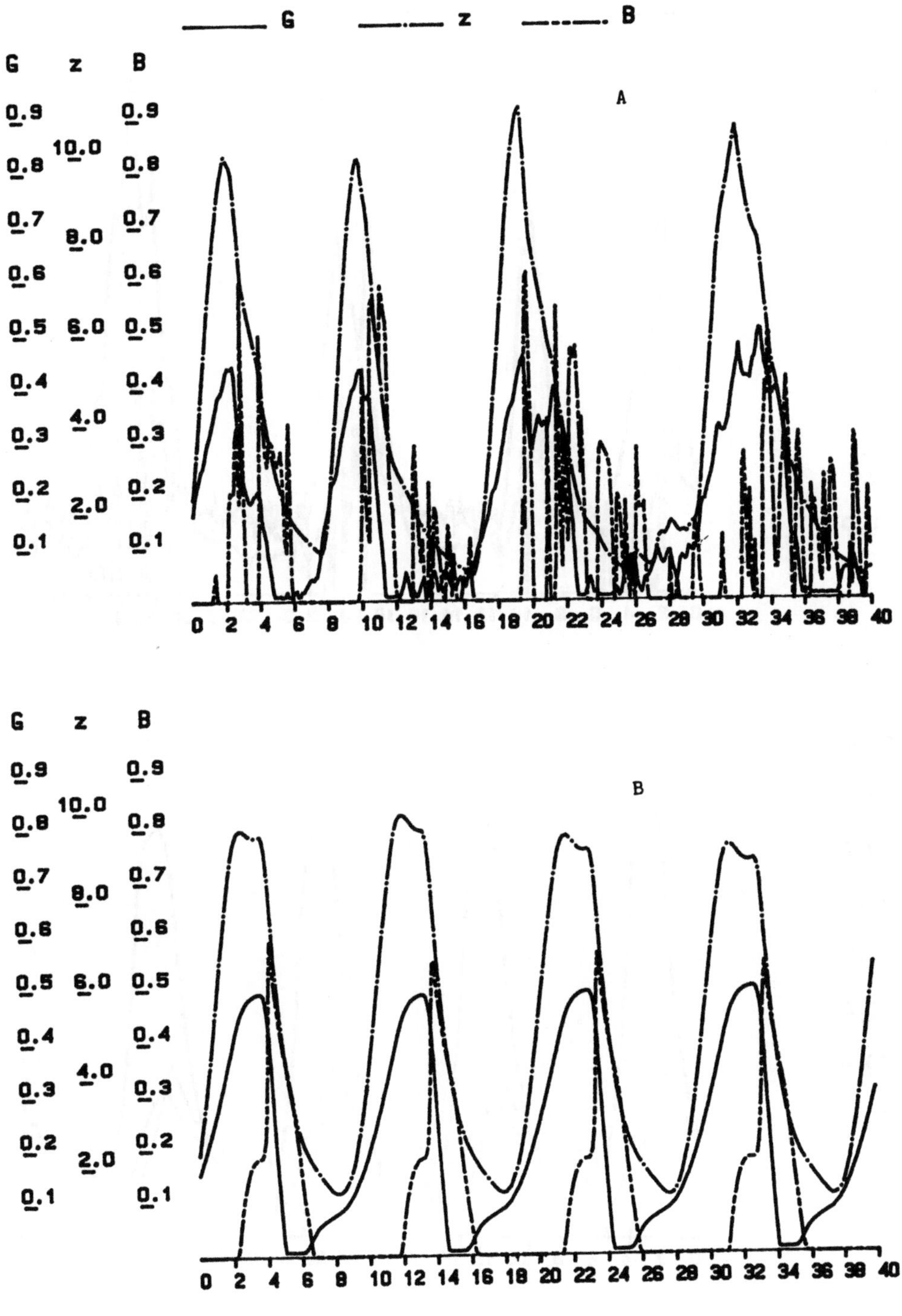

Fig 7.2. A (top) Stochastic, B (bottom) deterministic simulation. Desired investment fraction G, activity level z (million pounds/annum), bankruptcy rate B (per year); vs. time.

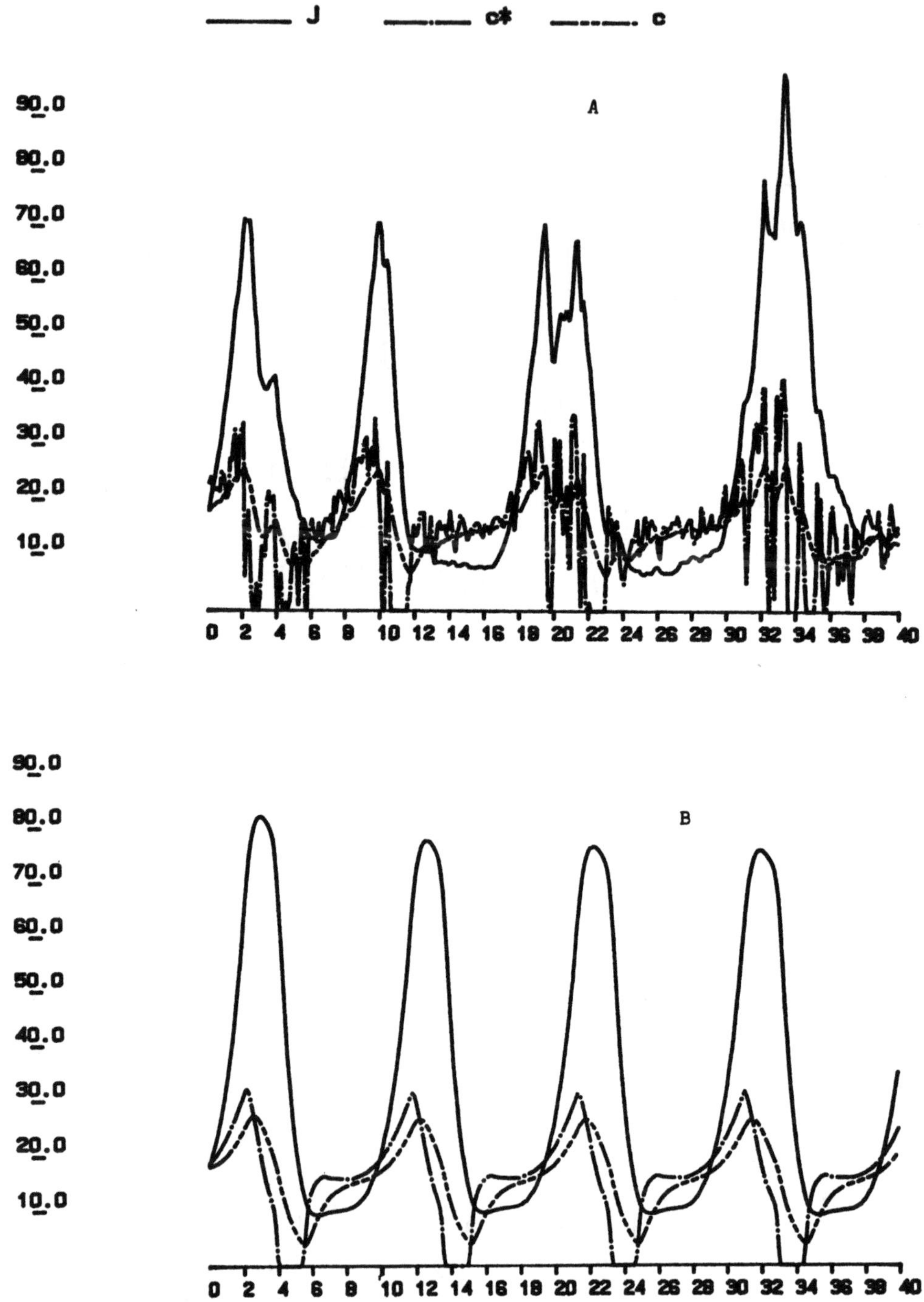

Fig. 7.3. A (top) Stochastic, B (bottom) deterministic simulation. Total investment J (million pounds), desired (c*) and actual (c) consumption (million pounds/annum); vs. time.

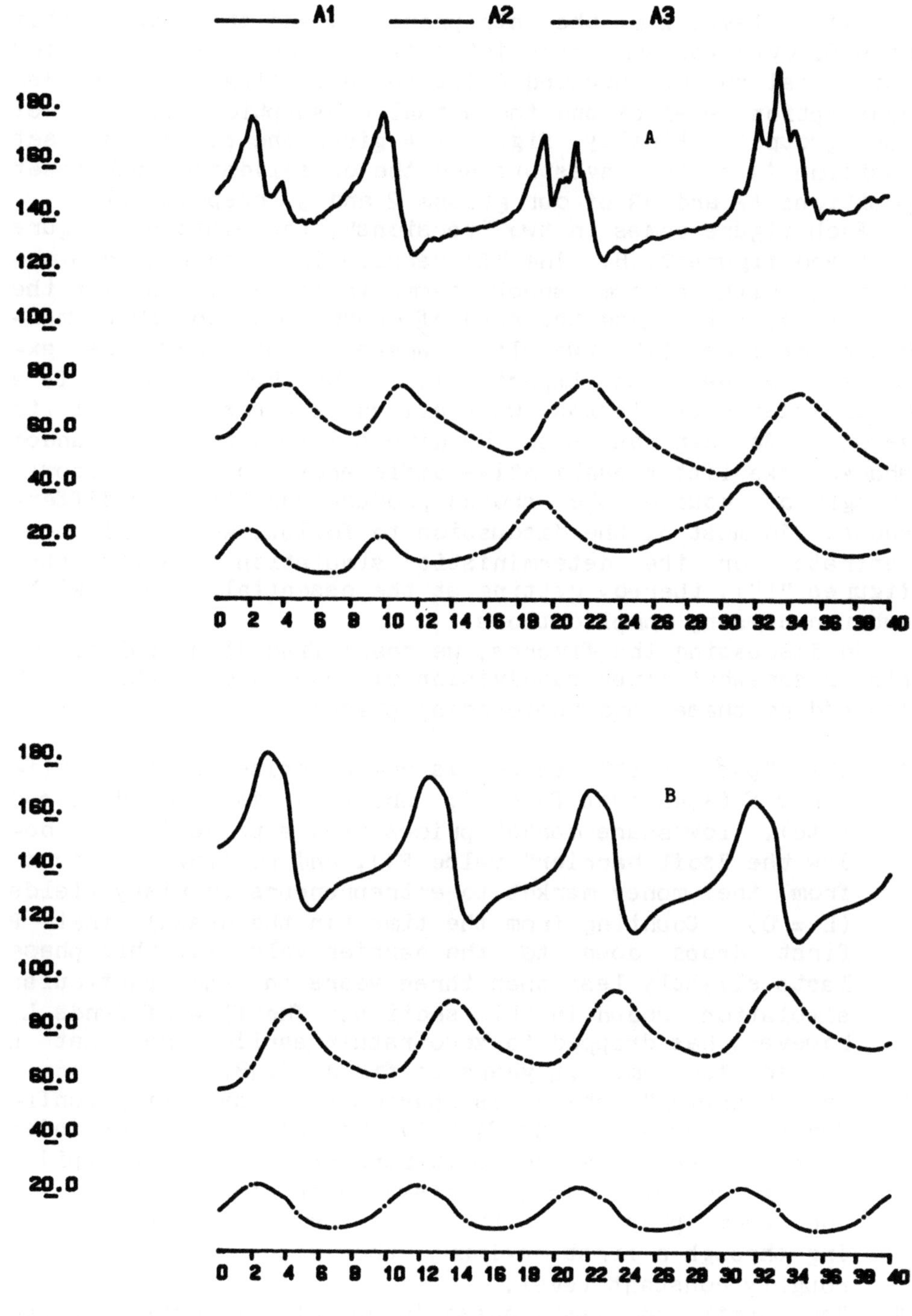

Fig. 7.4. A (top) Stochastic, B (bottom) deterministic simulation. Perceived assets of group 1 A1, cash assets of group 2 A2, indicator of group 3 assets A3 (million pounds); vs. time.

activity level z of the entrepreneurs, and their bankruptcy rate B, over the same time interval. Figure 7.3 contains the total amount invested J (at current valuation), the de- consumption level c* and the actual consumption level c of our group 1. Finally, figure 7.4 gives the perceived asset position A1 of the investors and the consolidated cash asset positions A2 and A3 of our groups 2 and 3, respectively.

Each figure comes in two "versions", for example, figure 7.1A and figure 7.1B. The "A" version is a stochastic simulation, with random shock terms in the equations for the bankruptcy rate B and the rate of change D of the share market price index (the two places where random shocks are expected to be most important). The "B" version is a deterministic simulation, with all shock terms set equal to zero. As can be seen by direct inspection, the random shocks make little **qualitative** difference to the outcome, though of course the shocks produce quantitative differences. In most of the discussion to follow, we shall concentrate on the deterministic simulation results (the figures "B"), thereby getting at the essential results without unnecessary complications.

In discussing the figures, we shall find it useful to employ a somewhat finer subdivision of one cycle than just "ascending phase" and "descending phase":

1. The "post-crash" phase is characterized by low confidence f (such that $fj < 1$, where j is the dividend rate), low share market prices (share price index P below the "soft barrier" value P1), and no flow of funds from the money market to entrepreneurs in risky fields ($L = 0$). Counting from the time (in the crash) that P first drops down to the barrier value P1, this phase lasts slightly less than three years in the particular simulation shown in this section. The flow of funds L, however, has dropped to zero rather earlier, so that L is zero for some 3.6 years in figure 7.1B.
2. The "upswing" phase is characterized by rising confidence f (now such that $fj > 1$), rising share price index P (no longer below the "soft barrier" P1), and a rapidly rising flow of funds L to risky enterprises.
3. The "boom" phase is initiated by the flow of funds L going through a first maximum, thereafter maintaining a roughly constant level.
4. The fourth, and last, phase in our classification is the "crash". Confidence has dropped to the point where desired investment G*A1 is in line with actual investment

J. At this point, the flow of funds L drops extremely sharply, in a few months, all the way down to zero. The result is catastrophe. The bankruptcy rate B goes sky-high, confidence drops sharply, and the share market takes a nosedive.

Let us now discuss these results. Much of the discussion has been anticipated already, in earlier chapters. Our purpose now is not to repeat these qualitative remarks, but rather to see what new, more specific comments we can make about the nineteenth century trade cycle in the light of these simulations. Although the simulations are based on a very rough, schematic model, they do lead to some interesting insights.

1. The main "leading variable" appears to be the cash flow L to speculative enterprises. The statistical information which comes nearest to our L in concept is the total capital raised from new issues in the money market. L stays zero (or close to zero in the stochastic simulations) until the start of the "upswing" phase. The rising inflow of funds to the projects of group 2 is the direct cause of this upswing. Also, it is the behavior of L which heralds the onset of the "boom" phase (which starts when L reaches its first maximum), and of the "crash" phase (which starts when L drops to zero sharply). L is such a good "leading indicator" because the flow of funds L is the immediate cause of the change in real investment. The underlying basic cause, that is, the ebb and flow of confidence, is (unfortunately) harder to measure and is usually not measured at all, a most regrettable omission.
2. Note that the share market price index P is a much less effective indicator. The activities of the money market involve more than just raising new capital; indeed, that function tends to take second place to the function which Keynes calls a "casino". [9] During the crash, the share market price index P drops more slowly than the flow of funds L, and lags that drop. During the post-crash phase, the share market index first continues dropping below the "soft barrier" level (assumed to equal 0.8 in figure 7.1), then recovers slowly back up to that level. If one looks at the stochastic simu-

[9] Keynes 1936 p.159.

lation (figure 7.1A), this involves some rapid ups and downs of the share price index P. However, none of this busy speculative activity has much real significance for the trade cycle. The upswing phase is tied to the flow of funds L, not to the share price index P, and the economic upswing only commences when L starts rising systematically and significantly.

3. The confidence variable f (figure 7.1) is the basic cause of it all. The upswing phase commences when confidence has recovered to the point at which fj = 1. Then and only then does L start rising sharply. Note also that f does not keep rising along with the share market price index P, at least not all the time. In particular, during the boom phase, the share market index P keeps rising until very close to the crash, whereas the confidence variable f reaches its maximum much earlier.
4. The chain of causation of boom and crash in our model is therefore as follows:
   a. During the upswing, confidence f and flow of funds L both rise, the latter very sharply.
   b. As both desired investment G*A1 and actual investment J rise during the upswing, the investors (though still willing to purchase shares on a rising market) become less willing to keep buying shares at an ever-increasing rate. They already have a significant fraction of their total perceived wealth tied up in the money market. Desired and actual investment are now no longer so far apart.
   c. In consequence, L does not continue to rise sharply but starts to level off. This results in a deterioration of the cash position A2 of the speculative enterprises (see the plot of A2 in figure 7.4). The rise of A2 slows down during the boom phase, and soon becomes a (slow) fall.
   d. With A2 starting to fall, the bankruptcy rate B (figure 7.2) is no longer zero, but rises to a (fairly low) plateau value. This provides another "leading indicator": bankruptcies start rising well before the real crash. Considered merely as an indicator, this effect provides less of a lead than the peaking of the flow of funds L, which occurs about half a year earlier. However, the bankruptcy rate B is not just an indicator, it is itself a major link in the chain of cause and effect.

e. As bankruptcies commence, confidence f no longer keeps rising, but starts to drop, slowly but steadily (note that all this is occurring while the share market price index P is still definitely on the rise!).

f. This drop in confidence, in turn, slows down the rise of the desired investment fraction G and, with it, desired total investment G*A1. This now moves closer into line with actual investment J, and when the two curves cross each other, the flow of funds L drops sharply to zero. At this point, the crash has commenced.

g. With the "money tap" L turned off, the cash position A2 of our speculative entrepreneurs deteriorates sharply, thereby driving the bankruptcy rate B sky-high. This in turn makes confidence drop even more sharply.

5. The concatenation of circumstances during the crash looks at first sight like a recipe for irreversible disaster. Everything is dropping at once: confidence, share price index, flow of funds, desired investment fraction, etc. The only thing which is high is the bankruptcy rate. What saves this model (and, we believe, what saved the real economy of the nineteenth century) is the "lower barrier" effect on the share price index P, the feeling of increasing numbers of investors that the drop has gone far enough and will be reversed before long. This effect dominates the "post-crash" phase. Without it, or something like it, no bottom would be reached.

6. Another important factor is the limited drop of the confidence variable f during the crash itself. f drops, of course, but does not drop to zero, or even very much below the "break-even point" where $fj = 1$. The farther f drops during the crash, the more time is required for the subsequent recovery. In our simple model, the rise of f is assumed to proceed at the rate of one year for every year that has elapsed. In the simulation shown here, f drops to 6.5 at its lowest point. The break-even point is $f = 1/j = 8.33$, so that it takes at least [10] $8.33-6.5 = 1.83$ years for f to recover from its lowest point back to the level at which the upswing phase can start. If the crash causes f to drop much lower, the upswing phase is correspondingly retarded.

We suggest that, in this model and we believe also in the reality of the nineteenth century economy, any policy designed to "smooth out" the crash would have been counterproductive. Most such policies tend to spread out the crash over a longer time interval, thereby allowing confidence to drop further - and therefore (!) retarding the subsequent upswing. If it was impossible to avoid the trade cycle altogether within the nineteenth century system (as we believe) then efforts to "alleviate" it, "smooth" it out, etc., should have been extremely dangerous. [11] Note however that these remarks apply to a **truly laissez-faire** system, such as that of the nineteenth century. They do **not** apply to the twentieth century situation with its many elements of state intervention, monopoly and oligopoly, trade union power, etc.

We conclude this section on the appearance of the cycle by emphasizing several points of agreement with experience:

1. The first, and most striking, success of the new approach is the extremely sharp "crash" which terminates the upward phase of the cycle. **No other model of the trade cycle reproduces this feature.**
2. The "bunching" of bankruptcies, that is, the very sharp peak in the bankruptcy rate B during the "panic". This is a well-known phenomenon, which is not reproduced by alternative trade cycle theories.
3. The activity level z of group 2 drops very sharply during the crash (primarily because bankruptcies are causing large-scale cessation of activities), and keeps dropping throughout the "post-crash" phase. z recovers only when funds start flowing once more to speculative enterprises (when L becomes positive again). Then the activity level rises sharply, following the rise of L but with a time delay. This very sharp variation in real investment activity over the course of the cycle (the maximum of z in figure 7.2B is more than six times (!) the minimum) and the bunching of this activity dur-

[10] This is a lower bound, not the actual value. When f reaches its minimum, the bankruptcy rate B is not yet down to zero, so that the true rate of rise of f is less than unity for some further time into the post-crash phase.
[11] Of course, nineteenth century British governments did not even contemplate such non-laissez-faire policies.

ing the boom phase is exactly what is observed (Matthews 1959).

In figure 2.2 (see page 14) we have plotted the rate of orders at the Baldwin locomotive works from 1872 to 1890. Although we have made no attempt at data fitting, and have selected our parameters and initial conditions without regard to figure 2.2, it is interesting to compare it with our variable z. Therefore we have drawn the z plot from figure 7.2B onto figure 2.2 (the dotted line on that figure). [12] In our opinion, allowing for the violent fluctuations in orders at the Baldwin works, which are possibly due to the size of the sample, the curves match remarkably well.

4. The index of share prices P also behaves in line with experience: The index keeps dropping (with random ups and downs, of course) for some time into the post-crash phase of the cycle. Then P turns up, but nothing much happens until later, after confidence has recovered to the point at which fj = 1. Then and only then does the increase become faster and more pronounced, giving rise to the upswing phase proper. The apparently aimless churning about of the money market for several years after a crash is a well-known phenomenon, for which other theories of the trade cycle provide no explanation.

[12] The identity of the vertical scales for the two plots is a coincidence.

CHAPTER VIII: The Longer Run

In this chapter, we shall investigate, to the extent that it is possible to do so with our highly simplified model, what happens over the longer run, that is, over a succession of cycles rather than just during one cycle.

Warning: This whole complex of arguments can not possibly be understood by using equilibrium concepts, concepts which are of course inapplicable to this model. There exists a misconception to the effect that a long term average over several complete cycles is equal to the result of an equilibrium calculation. This, unfortunately very common, belief is **false**.

SECTION A: GENERAL DISCUSSION.

During each cycle, there exist complicated flows of funds between the three groups.

1. Between groups 1 and 2, there is a flow of investment funds L in one direction, and of dividend payments jJ in the reverse direction.
2. Similarly, funds flow in both directions between groups 2 and 3. Group 2 pays for raw materials and labor, and group 3 pays rental for the use of capital equipment.
3. Finally, there is a flow of funds between group 1 and group 3. Payments for rental of land go one way. In the reverse direction there are payments by the landed gentry, for consumption goods.

The balance between these various flows alters sharply as the trade cycle passes through its various phases. Consequently, **there is no "normal rate of return"**: actual returns to investors vary violently during the cycle.

In the simulations shown so far, the investors (group 1) are the main losers, and group 3 is the main beneficiary. The reason is that the investors overestimate their true income (they count unrealized capital gains on the share market as "income") and hence spend too freely during the upswing and boom phases of the cycle. This appears to be what actually happened in the nineteenth century.

However, within our model, this outcome depends sensitively on the parameters chosen within the model equations, in particular those parameters which determine the rental for land and the desired consumption expenditures of the investor class (the parameters v', k' and k"). By altering the values of these parameters, we can make either group 1 or group 3 become the main "loser" in the economic contest, as judged by performance over several cycles. To this extent, then, our model does not allow a clear theoretical conclusion.

However, there is another way of looking at this situation. In order for an economic system to continue functioning indefinitely, no group can be a significant net loser in the long term. If there is such a group, then it must, after a number of cycles, go bankrupt altogether. When that happens, the structure of the economic system changes altogether, so that the model equations no longer apply. [1]

This condition, that no group be a significant net loser over the cycle, is extremely difficult to satisfy in the model as specified so far. In order to satisfy this condition, the various parameters must be chosen "just right", in a correct relationship to one another. In the simulations shown here, we have chosen our parameters close to (but not precisely equal to) this "correct" relationship.

However, such a "correct" (or nearly correct) choice is most unlikely to be achieved in any actual economy, for the following reasons:

1. The parameters in question describe the economic behavior of different groups, groups that have no short-run interest in coordinating their various demands.
2. "Wrong" behavior does not result in immediate, or even short-run, evil effects. Rather, these effects of imbalance show up only as a result of several complete trade cycles. Even with the best will in the world (which was not present) the causal link between these behavioral parameters and the long-run stagnation of one or another part of the economy should have been most difficult to discern.
3. Economic theory proved another severe hindrance to intelligent adjustment of conflicting claims. Economic theory in the middle of the nineteenth century was dominated completely by the thought of Ricardo. Ricardo was a firm believer in Say's Law, and asserted forcefully

[1] This situation is closely analogous to the extinction of species in theoretical ecology, see May 1973.

> that a "general glut" was simply impossible. The fact that such gluts were occurring right in front of his eyes never disturbed such an abstract theorist as Ricardo. With accepted economic theory denying the very existence of the phenomenon which needed to be understood, and insisting on using (inapplicable) equilibrium concepts instead, it proved impossible to even ask the right questions.

Let us see, therefore, whether our model can be modified so as to make the conditions for survival of the economy less stringent and easier to satisfy.

SECTION B: THE MONEY SUPPLY.

One property of our model, as specified so far, is that it yields a constant money supply, at least as far as transactions between our three groups are concerned. This mathematically demonstrable property corresponds to the fact that there was a strict metallic based currency throughout the century, together with a non-discretionary rule (Peel's bank act) for the issue of secondary currency (bank notes).

Of course, we know that large volumes of commercial transactions in the nineteenth century were on credit, utilizing the instrument of bills of exchange. Furthermore, many writers [2] considered the contraction of this credit important in the business cycle.

In our model, all this is hidden in our group 3, "everyone else". This group includes the manufacturers, importers, wholesalers, retailers, bankers and laborers. The manufacturers, wholesalers and retailers can sell to each other using bills of exchange, or any other form of credit, without affecting our model.

While there is no doubt that contraction of commercial credit instruments played an important role in the course of the "crash", it is our view that this represents a secondary, later effect of an initial loss of confidence by group 1 in the future of the more speculative enterprises (our group 2). Once confidence is shaken in one area of the economy, a feeling of unease spreads over other areas as well. In a complete model, designed for econometric test-

[2] Bagehot, J.S. Mill, etc.

ing, we should have to include commercial credit, bills of exchange, and an explicit banking sector. For our cut-down, schematic model, however, we feel that they may be omitted.

Therefore, we have as a "constant of motion" of our model the money supply (gold and gold backed notes). Since we have included in the perceived assets of group 1 their share holdings J, our variable A1 is not confined to their currency holdings. The latter are given by the difference A1-J. The mathematical demonstration that the money supply (equal to A1-J+A2+A3 in our model) is constant in time, can be found in Boyd (1986).

This result implies that a delicate situation exists with regard to the currency holdings of the three groups. If any one group should succeed in increasing its liquid wealth, one or both of the other groups must lose liquidity. This makes the model, as specified so far, exceedingly sensitive and unlikely to yield long-term survival of the model economy.

A fact that nineteenth century men of affairs noticed was a correlation between long-run (over several cycles) prosperity or depression, and the flow of gold from gold mines. Between 1830 and 1850, roughly, there was a long-run depression. Then there was prosperity between 1850 (roughly) and 1873, followed by the "Great Depression" which lasted into the 1890's.

Empirically, there were major gold finds (in California and in Australia, among others) just before 1850, resulting in a major inflow of gold.

That the money supply did grow due to the exogenous effects of gold discoveries is historical fact. The extent of that growth was at times enormous:

> "At a time when the world's monetary stock of gold (apart from hoards in the East) was estimated at little more than 200,000,000 pounds sterling, the annual output suddenly rose in 1853 to 31,000,000 pounds sterling, and from 1860 to 1890 settled down at something well over 20,000,000 with a slight tendency to fall off in the latter part of the period." [3]

Taking these rough figures, the gold supply grew by 15.5% in the single year 1853, yet in 1872 the rate of growth had

[3] Hawtrey 1938 p.46.

fallen to less than 3% per annum, and continued to decline as a percentage rate.

In order to investigate longer term evolution, we suggest that we should add to the model equations, an inflow of "gold", that is, of pure purchasing power accruing to one or more groups, without compensating payments to anyone else.

SECTION C: EFFECTS OF AN INCREASE IN THE MONEY SUPPLY.

Let q stand for the rate at which new money is being produced. For simplicity, we assume that all this new money finds its way, in the first instance, into the pockets of group 1. This is hardly realistic, but it makes no difference for our present argument. We are interested, at the moment, only in long term averages over several cycles. Since money flows between our three groups at varying, but always significant, rates throughout each cycle, money collected at first by any one group is soon redistributed among all three groups.

We have therefore included, in the equation governing the time development of the perceived wealth of group 1, the term "+q" on the right hand side. [4]

In section B we noted that in 1853 the total gold in the world was estimated at 200,000,000 pounds sterling, with annual output of 31,000,000 pounds sterling. This output mainly originated from new gold finds in the last years of the 1840's. From 1860 to 1890 gold production settled at roughly 20 million pounds sterling per annum.

We have made our model's monetary unit equal to one million pounds sterling. [5] For simplicity, let us take gold mining as constant, and ignore the initial surge to 31 million pounds sterling. [6] In the simulations shown be-

---

[4] More precisely, this term appears in the equation defining the "perceived income" y of group 1, equation C.5. This y then enters the equation for d(A1)/dt, equation C.11.

[5] The choice of monetary unit in the model is arbitrary. All those variables and parameters with dimension of an economic value or a value flow can be rescaled by a common factor, without altering the simulations.

[6] We wish to investigate the effects of gold mining, not of random shocks.

low, we let q be a constant equal to 20 (20 million pounds per annum). [7]

In figures 8.1A-8.4A we show the course of the model (deterministic), over a longer time than figures 7.1-7.4, with money input at this rate. Note that we had to enlarge the scale greatly for all variables with a component of money value in their dimension. For comparison, in figures 8.1B-8.4B we show the same run as in figures 7.1B-7.4B (i.e., no input of new money), but drawn to the new scale and time period.

The first striking point to note is that the booms are initially vastly higher (look at z, J, L) than in the constant money supply case. As our assumed constant money input becomes less and less as a percentage of total money stock, the booms then decline in height.

However, this decline is not steady. Subsequent peaks do not decrease smoothly, but instead the model jumps suddenly to a cycle of lower amplitude. Furthermore, at a later stage it briefly jumps back again to the larger cycle. From observed experience, we do sometimes get a much larger cycle in the real economy, and also periods such as the great depression from 1873 to 1896, when "A bicycle boom was about the most exciting." [8] This suggests that the great depression was due, at least in part, to the relative reduction in the rate of growth of the money supply.

A second point is that, although within our crude model the money input was assigned initially to the investor class, the greater part of the new money has ended up in the hands of the other two groups. Although A3 starts out way

---

[7] Although the currency was based on gold, q does not equal the rate at which gold is being mined, because: (1) Some of the newly mined gold did not flow to England, but (for example) into "hoards in the East". (2) As soon as gold entered the vaults of the Bank of England, the Bank could, and did, issue additional currency in the form of banknotes, in a predetermined ratio. We note that these two effects tend to cancel each other.

[8] See Rostow 1948 for the quotation. It is possible that the sudden jumps from one type of cyclical behavior to another, and then back, are related to the mathematical property known as "strange attractors". We have not investigated this, because (1) the model equations are very complicated, mathematically speaking, and yet (2) they are too simple and schematic, economically speaking.

below A1, it very soon climbs above it. [9] Money in the hands of group 1 encourages them to invest more and so transfer more of their capital to group 2, who then spend it on bigger and better railways, canals and other projects. Of course, the investors are still doing well out of the gold mining, but they are definitely falling behind in this "class struggle".

We note that this new money does (in our model) end up in the hands of group 3 rather than group 2. However the total wealth of group 2, as distinct from their liquid assets A2, would include the assets from their completed projects. Furthermore, our assumptions about group 3, in particular the assumption that they pay a "rental for capital" of a4*(c+z), are over simplified for this type of study. In actual fact, as group 3 gets wealthier, its own consumption increases and changes form towards including more manufactured and luxury goods. This requires more capital to produce so that this rental should increase much more than our model, designed mainly for phenomena on the time scale of one trade cycle, allows. Therefore, although we can conclude that the investors can not retain their money in the face of the trade cycle mechanism, we can not be sure where this money will end up, other than that it goes into productive activity of some sort.

[9] Redistribution between these groups can be achieved also by altering model parameters (for example k') without introducing new money input. However, in that case the improved position of one group is bought at the expense of losses in one or both of the other groups. This is an essential difference.

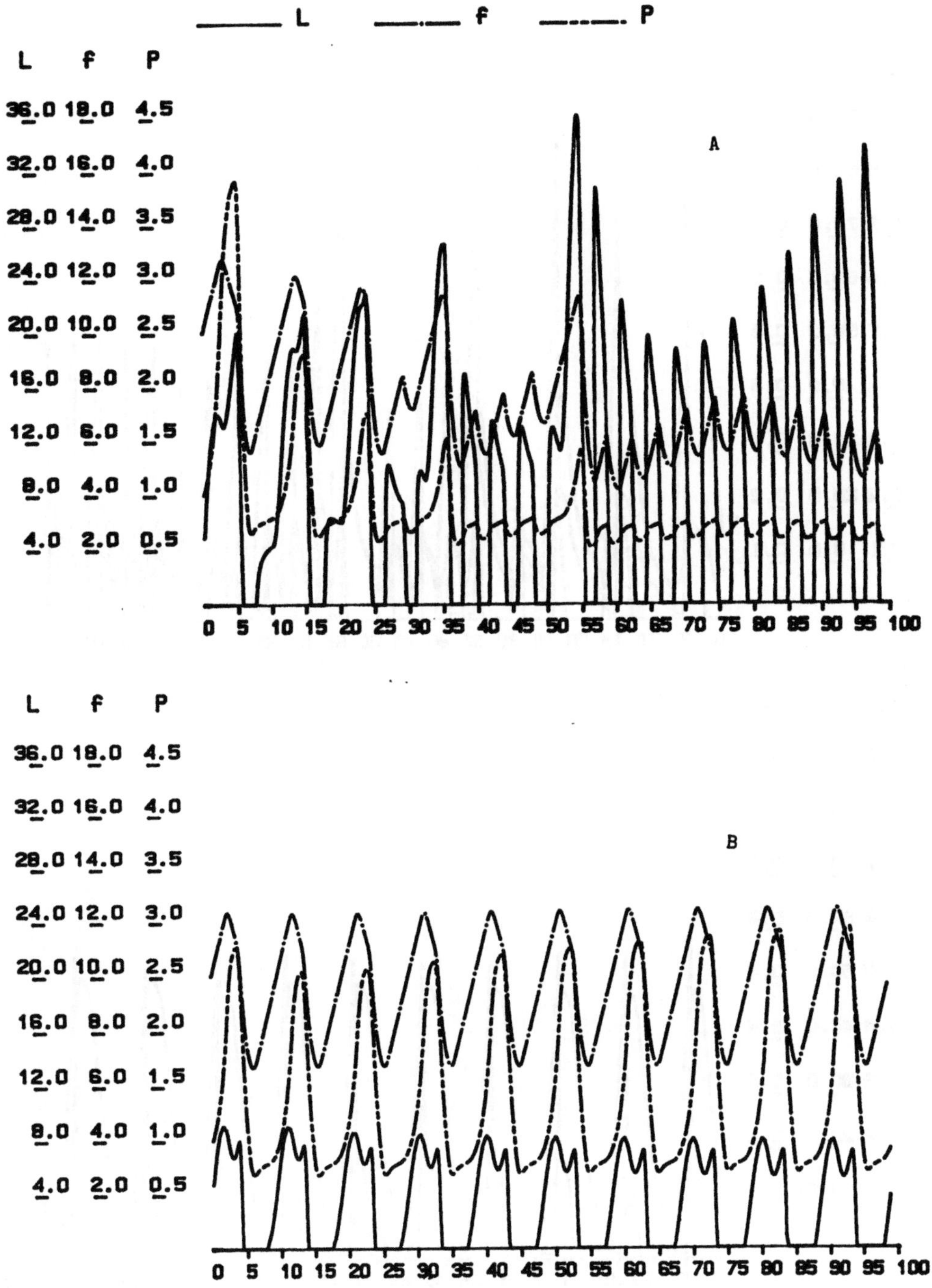

Fig. 8.1. Deterministic simulations. A (top) expanding money supply, B (bottom) constant money supply. Confidence f (years), share price index P, flow of funds to speculative enterprises L (million pounds/annum); vs. time (years). The "constant money supply" graphs are as in Fig. 7.1B, only the scales are different.

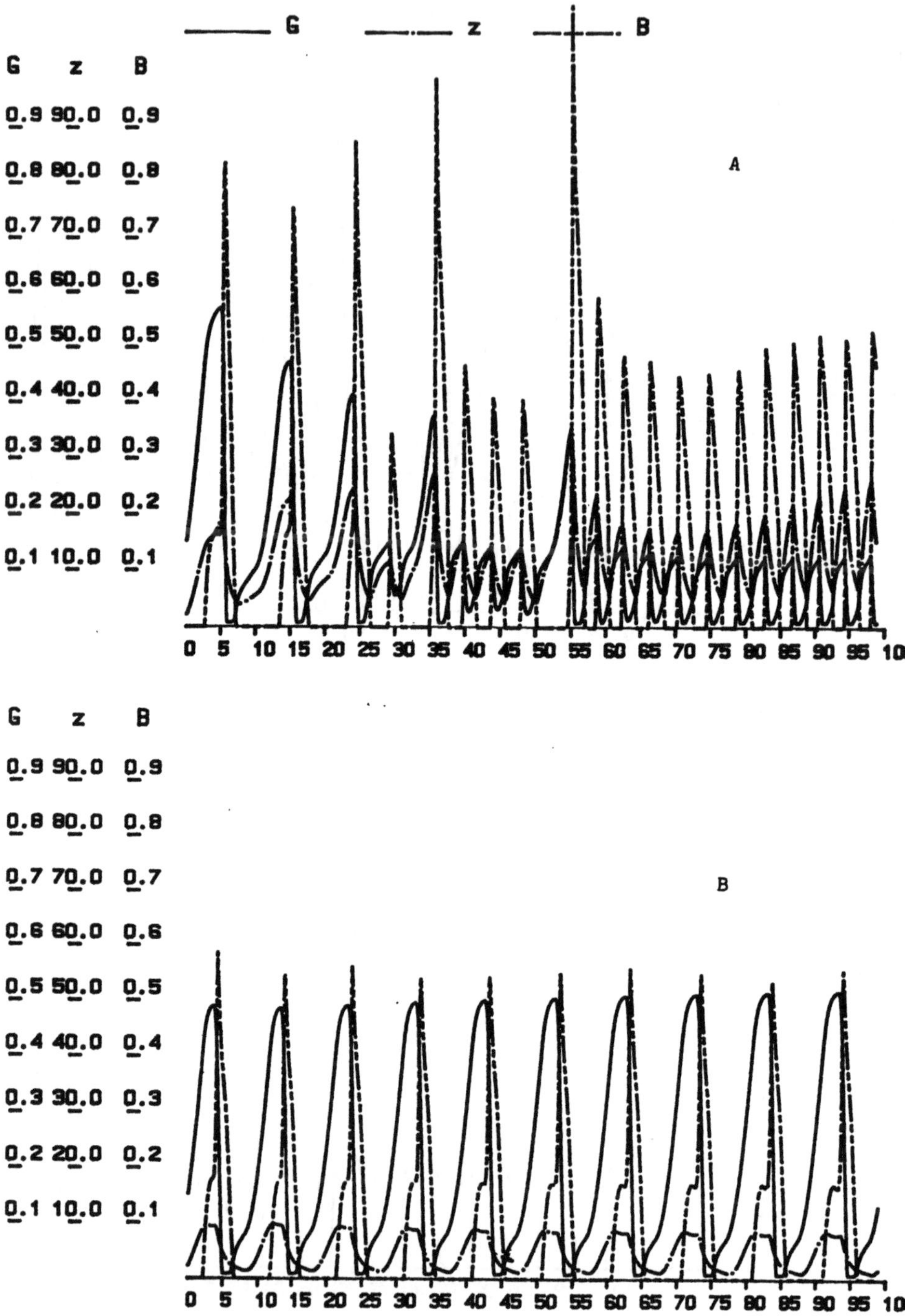

Fig. 8.2. Deterministic simulations. A (top) expanding money supply, B (bottom) constant money supply. Desired investment fraction G, activity level z (million pounds/annum), bankruptcy rate B (per annum); vs. time (years). The "constant money supply" graphs are as in Fig. 7.2B, only the scales are different.

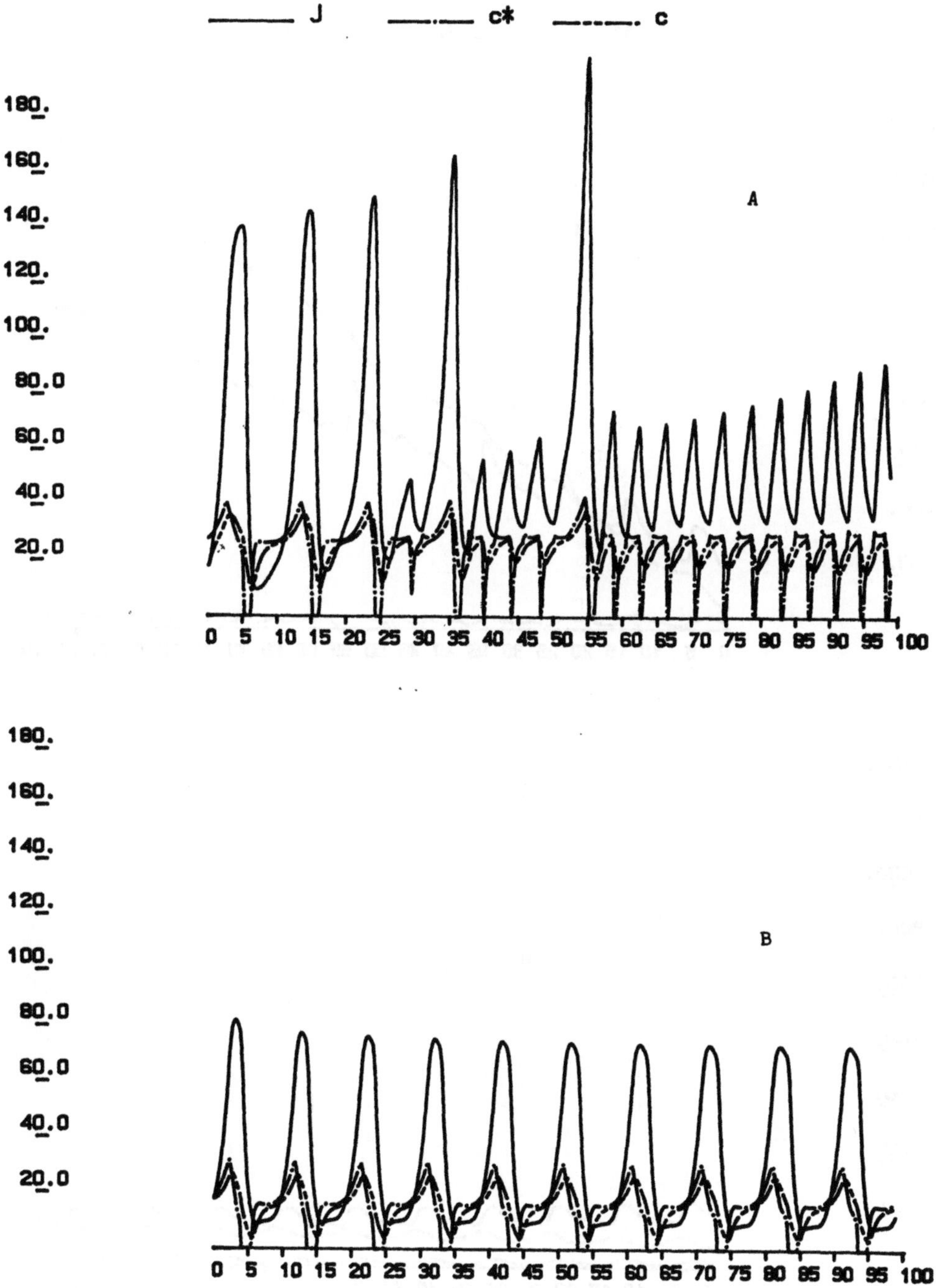

Fig. 8.3. Deterministic simulations. A (top) expanding money supply, B (bottom) constant money supply. Value of total investment J (million pounds), desired (c*) and actual (c) consumption (million pounds/annum); vs. time (years). The "constant money supply" graphs are as in Fig. 7.3B, only the scales are different.

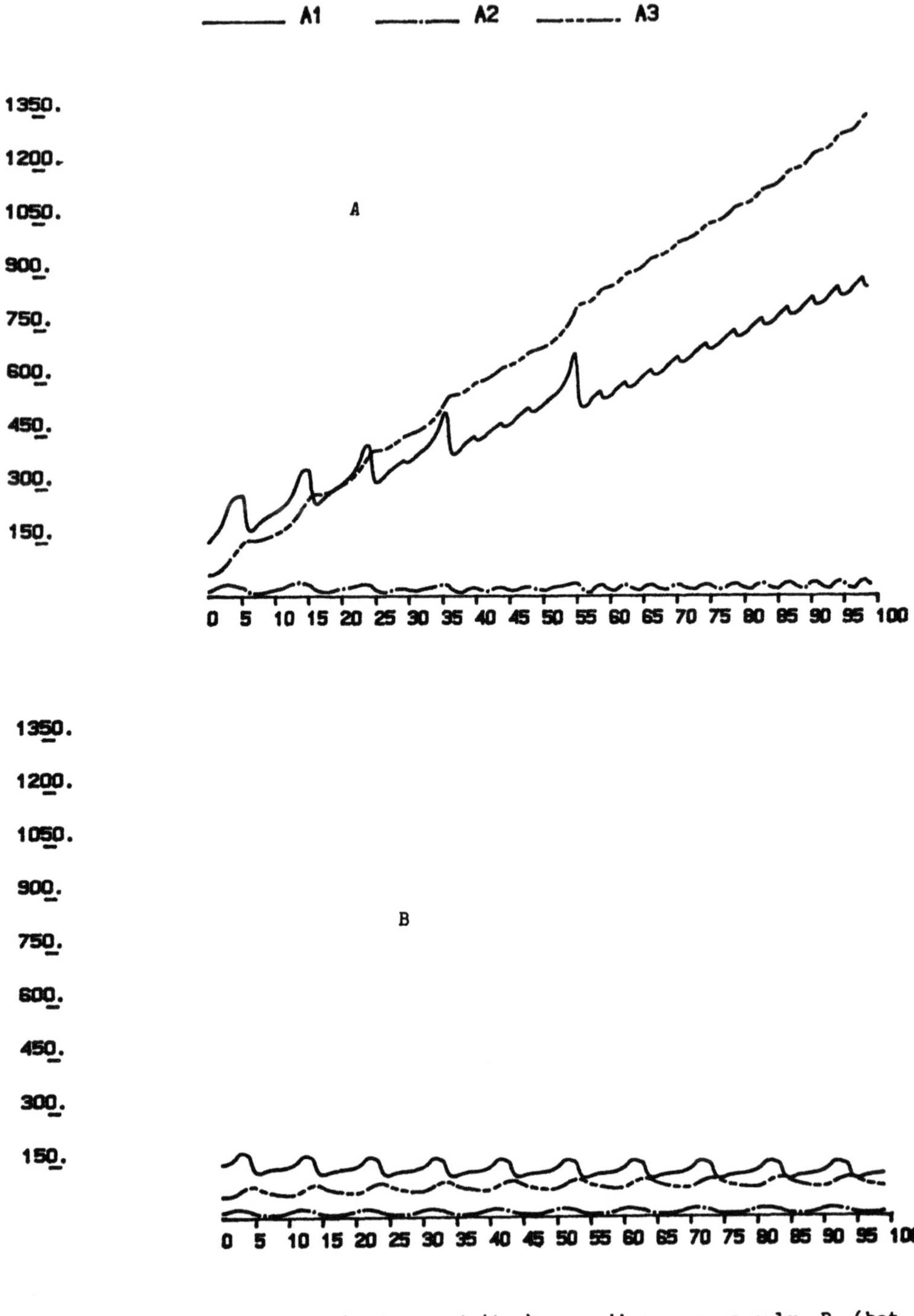

Fig. 8.4. Deterministic simulations. A (top) expanding money supply, B (bottom) constant money supply. Perceived assets of group 1 A1, cash assets of group 2 A2, indicator of group 3 assets A3 (million pounds); vs. time (years). The "constant money supply" graphs are as in Fig. 7.4B, only the scales are different.

CHAPTER IX: Some General Remarks

SECTION A: THE ECONOMIC FUNCTION OF THE TRADE CYCLE.

Let us ask what economic function, if any, was performed by this continuing series of violent oscillations of the economic system of the nineteenth century. One might think (and many people, then and now, do think) that it should be much better to have a smoother-running system, not subject to such dreadful cataclysms every nine or ten years.

We would like to suggest that this conclusion is by no means certain. If regularity of operation of the economic system (the usual term is "stabilization") is all that is wanted, then there exist many historical instances of "stable" economic systems for our inspection. Indeed, for thousands upon thousands of years of recorded human history, economic change is exceedingly slow, almost invisible on the scale of a human life. Only wars and natural disasters produce any changes in such essentially static economies.

For a particularly instructive comparison, consider eighteenth century France and eighteenth century Britain. In France, the panic of 1720, resulting from the "Mississippi bubble" of John Law, was remembered throughout the century with vivid horror. The authoritarian government of the ancien regime made sure that such a thing could not happen again. Speculation was controlled tightly, so no successors to John Law could arise. By contrast, eighteenth century Britain was, for long periods on end, controlled by a Whig government friendly to commercial interests. Speculation was not encouraged, but neither was it forbidden.

The results from these opposite policies were striking. In Britain, there was a series of ups and downs, with "panics" at more or less regular intervals. The British economy was "unstable", but on a secular scale it grew by leaps and bounds (literally!) throughout the eighteenth century. By contrast, the French economy of the ancien regime behaved in an orderly, regular and controlled fashion. No violent ups and downs, no wild booms or even wilder panics, disturbed its stately and inexorable descent into the ultimate disaster of 1789!

We conclude that "stability", by itself, should not be considered the main or ultimate goal of economic management. Stability is, all too often, merely stagnation.

It is natural to ask whether this apparent correlation between economic instability and economic progress is a complete accident, or whether perhaps the trade cycle serves a real economic function. Our model suggests that the latter is the correct answer. Our group 1, the investors, is basically parasitical on the rest of the economy. These "investors" collect rent for land, but do not perform any significant economic service in return for these payments.

It is evident that no industrial economy can develop beyond a certain point until it possesses adequate capital goods capacity. But it is also evident that under conditions of private enterprise the extremely costly capital investment necessary for much of this development is not likely to be undertaken for the same reason as the industrialization of cotton or other consumer goods. For these a mass market already exists, at least potentially: even very primitive men wear shirts and use household equipment.

The problem is how to put a sufficiently vast market sufficiently quickly within the purview of businessmen. No such ready-made market exists, e.g., for heavy iron equipment such as girders. It only comes into existence in the course of an industrial revolution (and not always then), and those who lock up their money in the very heavy investments required even by quite modest ironworks (compared to quite large cotton-mills) before the market for their products is visibly there, are more likely to be speculators, adventurers, dreamers, or gullible fools, than to be sound businessmen.

If the investors retain their rents, hoarding them or spending them only on luxury consumption and/or war, then funds which could be used for investment and economic development are frittered away idly. From this point of view, there is a definite advantage to the economy as a whole in any scheme, no matter how unstable or fraudulent, which can persuade these investors to release some of their wealth for the purpose of real investment in productive activity.

The trade cycle, in our view, acts as such a scheme. Furthermore, we assert that the associated instability and recurring panics are a necessary element for the success of that scheme.

Let us elucidate this second point. In order to persuade the investors to invest, they have to be promised sky-high returns, and the money market must appear to bring enormous (and hence quite unrealizable) capital gains. This requirement ensures that a crash has to come sooner or later. In the crash, many investors lose their investment. The net result is a transfer of funds from the investor class to the class of industrialists, and to some elements of the general population.

Naturally, industrialists go bankrupt in a panic, too, lots of them. However, the **class** of industrialists gains. An enterprise which goes bankrupt is bought up, for a song, by some other industrialist. [1] It is not bought by some member of group 1, who after all should not know what to do with his purchase. Thus, the overall result is that money invested by the investor class shows up, after the panic, in the form of actual productive capacity in the hands of the industrial class. The factory or other project may be only partially completed, but that is unimportant.

From this economic point of view, the vast expense of speculative manias such as the railway booms, is their chief advantage. No doubt in the long run, the capacity of the railways to open up areas hitherto cut off by high transport costs from the world market, and the vast increase in the speed, bulk and reliability of overland communication, are going to be major factors. However, in the first half of the nineteenth century railways themselves are economically unimportant - outside Britain railways are few; in Britain no point is more than 70 miles from the sea, and all the chief industrial areas of the nineteenth century, with one exception, are either on the sea or within easy reach of it. From our perspective, the immense appetite of the railways firstly for investment capital and following this for iron and steel, for coal, for heavy machinery, and for labor, is more important. This provides just that massive demand which is needed to transform the capital goods industries in the industrial revolution.

In our view, it is this net transfer of funds away from a class of economic parasites, to an economically productive class, which is the positive contribution of the nineteenth century trade cycle. To the extent that "stability" is equivalent to "stagnation", even a violent trade cycle is preferable in the long run. [2]

Note that, on this interpretation, the trade cycle can serve its economic function only if its operation is not understood by the main economic actors, in particular not by the investors who are its destined victims. Whether deliberate or accidental, the persistent failure of nineteenth century economic theory to elucidate the mechanism causing

---

[1] Pigou 1927 p.87.

[2] Provided, that is, that the observers live a century later, so that they do not themselves fall victim to the short run effects!

the trade cycle proved of great help to the fortunes of the entrepreneurial class.

SECTION B: EXPLOITATION.

In section 4D, we discussed models of the Goodwin type. These models start from the ideas of Karl Marx on the causation of trade cycles. In our view, some essential elements of the puzzle have been omitted in models of this type. These elements are:

1. Investor confidence, or its converse, uncertainty of the future.
2. The distinction between our groups 1 and 2, i.e., between what we may call "rentiers" and "entrepreneurs".

In our view, these omissions are related directly to the underlying Marxian approach.

First, Marx's theory of value and surplus value (the labor theory of value) has no room for subjective, psychological factors such as confidence. Thus, while Marx, an astute observer of the economic scene, is very much aware of "confidence" and share market speculation, his own theoretical framework makes it difficult, if not impossible, for him to do much more than mention such things on the side. A "value" not based upon labor time is, for Marx, a contradiction in terms.

The second omission is the distinction between "rentiers" and "entrepreneurs". The two main classes in these Marx-based models are labor and capital, the exploited and the exploiters; subdivisions within the exploiting class hardly matter.

There is no doubt that labor was exploited very badly in the nineteenth century. However, exploitation per se runs throughout the history of the human race, with pitifully few exceptions. Exploitation is too universal and prevalent to explain very much. In the nineteenth century, Russian serfs were exploited at least as viciously as British "free" laborers. Yet the Russian economy remained backward throughout that period, quite unlike the British economy.

The Russian exploiting class squeezed their serfs mercilessly, but (on the whole, with individual exceptions of course) did not invest the proceeds, but rather spent them on luxury consumption and idle show. If the returns from exploitation are frittered away in this fashion, then the economy can not grow. To achieve economic growth, it is necessary to persuade the exploiters to forego personal consumption in favor of investment.

However, as Keynes pointed out so forcefully: [3]

> "Enterprise only pretends to itself to be mainly actuated by the statements in its own prospectus, however candid and sincere. Only a little more than an expedition to the South Pole, is it based on an exact calculation of benefits to come. Thus if the animal spirits are dimmed and the spontaneous optimism falters, leaving us to depend on nothing but a mathematical expectation, enterprise will fade and die ... "

Without "animal spirits", there is no progress.

At this point, however, one must distinguish sharply between entrepreneurs, who can reasonably be expected to possess an adequate supply of animal spirits, and rentiers who are, almost by definition, low in animal spirits (particularly as regards investment in areas other than agriculture). Yet just these rentiers (nineteenth century British landed gentlemen as well as Russian noblemen) are among the primary and immediate recipients of Marxian surplus value, in the form of rents.

One problem of growth is therefore: how to persuade wealthy and selfish men to hand over real entitlement to immediate luxury consumption, in exchange for mere paper promises. It would not do to really recompense the rentiers out of future income, to make good on these promises, in full. To the extent that the rentiers are repaid, the problem has not been solved at all, merely postponed a bit.

The answer is to promise them the moon in future dividends, and to make sure that, in the meantime, share "values" on the exchange keep rising, so that the occasional sceptic can sell his shares at a profit, thereby assuring all the other investors that their "values" are safe and sound. When the inevitable crash comes, all these "values" turn into so many scraps of paper. The rentiers have been expropriated, and growth has been financed by their, entirely involuntary and unanticipated, sacrifice.

[3] Keynes 1936 p.161-162.

SECTION C: IMPLICATIONS FOR ECONOMIC THEORY.

Finally, let us explore some of the implications of our model for current economic theory.

The most important, and perhaps the most controversial, implication is that "equilibrium is blither". [4] Roy Harrod [5] was completely right about the equilibrium system (not the actual economy!) being "balanced on a knife-edge". This knife-edge balance is of no interest, since it can not last.

What the economy actually does is unrelated to this purely theoretical equilibrium state. Rather, a laissez-faire economy goes through an endogenous, self-sustained oscillation which nearly (though not precisely) repeats itself time and again. [6]

At any given time, there may be "equilibrium" in the trivial short-run sense of markets clearing; indeed, in our model, this condition is obeyed by most of the endogenous variables; the others deviate from this short-run condition only to the limited extent that there are delayed adjustments of actual values to "desired" or "predicted" values.

What is **false** is that this model economy, or the real laissez-faire economy, is in **long-run** equilibrium, or in any state even vaguely similar to long-run equilibrium. The actual, endogenous, self-limiting cycle is inherent in the normal functioning of the system. It is affected somewhat, but is not changed profoundly, by random shocks. It continues to exist even in the complete absence of such shocks.

The trade cycle is the normal mode of functioning of a laissez-faire economic system, not some kind of "aberration" or deviation from a (supposedly normal) state of equilibrium or balanced growth.

Any attempt to abolish this cycle by governmental controls on speculation (such as existed in eighteenth century

[4] J. M. Keynes, quoted by: Shackle 1974, p.38.

[5] Harrod 1939, 1948.

[6] Unfortunately, there does not appear to exist a suitable mathematical theory of such "almost repeating" cycles. The concept called a "limit cycle" of a non-linear system comes closest to what we need here, but fails to allow for small, systematic deviations from perfect periodicity. We also mention that "strange attractors" do not model what we need here.

France) prevents the system from functioning normally, and is very likely to lead to secular stagnation of the economy.

This provides a changed view of the task of economic theory. No longer is it sufficient to start from economic equilibrium and tack on economic dynamics as an afterthought. With an endogenous cycle in operation, equilibrium analysis is logically invalid, and leads to conclusions which are incorrect theoretically as well as misleading practically. [7]

We believe that we have made a modest start in this book, but a great deal more remains to be done. Here is a field wide open for economic theorists. We hope that at least some of those who have read this far will take up the challenge to go further.

[7] This paragraph assumes that economic theory aims to explain actual economic events, and to aid us in bettering economic performance. However, this is not the only conceivable aim. The Roman Catholic Church uses the term "apologetics" to mean a set of writings which purport to give logical reasons for acceptance of the dogmas of the Catholic faith. If economic theory is intended primarily as apologetics, in this sense, for laissez-faire policies by the State, then current economic theory is already very well adapted to that purpose. Improvement of that theory should then be neither necessary nor desirable; it might even be impossible.

APPENDIX A: **Asymmetry of the Cycle**

In this appendix we present the details of our test of asymmetry between ascending and descending phases of the trade cycle, and we discuss, briefly, some other work in the literature.

We wish to concentrate on an economic quantity which is strongly connected with business cycles, and for which there are good data extending over a long period. Pig iron production in the U.S.A. is such a quantity. The data are excellent. [1] According to Burns and Mitchell, [2] pig iron production exhibits perfect conformity between specific cycles and reference cycles. [3] The cyclical fluctuations are of pronounced amplitude, and the long term trend is well approximated by a simple smooth curve. [4] Burns and Mitchell obtain the following results for ascending and descending slopes, after "de-trending" the raw data over 15 full cycles for pig iron production, between March 1879 and March 1933:

average slope of upswing = 2.49
average slope of downswing = 4.02

The large discrepancy between slow upswing and fast downswing, if significant statistically, establishes the asymmetry of the cycle in pig iron production.

Before proceeding to establish the statistical significance of this discrepancy, and hence to draw our conclusion of asymmetry, we first deal with a criticism against this type of analysis made by Neftci: [5]

> "In testing for asymmetry over the business cycle, one may be tempted to divide the sample into two groups, one representing downturns, the other expansions; estimate two separate autoregressive representations for each subsample; and then, using any standard test, to see if the two sets of estimates are significantly different from each other. It turns out that, because the definition of asymmetry uses a sample path prop-

---

[1] Macauley 1938.
[2] Burns 1947, see Table 97 on p.291.
[3] "Specific cycles" are cycles in one particular economic variable. "Reference cycles" are coincident cycles in a large number of economic variables.
[4] This can be seen on chart 35, page 272 of Burns 1947.
[5] Neftci 1984 p.310.

erty of the series under consideration, this test will be biased: ... one increases the probability that the test will reject the null hypothesis - which in this case will be symmetric behavior."

This argument may appear compelling at first sight, but there are difficulties:

1. It is clear from simple symmetry considerations that the "bias", to the extent that it exists at all, is of a rather peculiar form: it is a bias against a finding of symmetry, but not a bias in a particular direction, i.e., there is no tendency to favor rapid downturns as against rapid upturns. Thus, if this problem should be serious, one should expect that tests of this sort, carried out on a number of different cyclical time series, should indicate asymmetry of both kinds, favoring rapid upturns for some of the series, rapid downturns for the remainder, in approximately equal proportions. This is the very opposite of what is observed: all such tests agree that the downslopes are rapid, the upslopes slow (for an example of this, see Table 4.1 at the end of chapter 4).
2. Neftci's own preferred procedure is not free from objections. In order to be able to carry out his technical statistical manipulations, Neftci states: "we have to impose further restrictions on the process". He assumes that the process is stationary and a second order Markov process. The argument given in favor of this assumption is hardly convincing, yet all the subsequent calculations depend on it. A Markov process is not, in our view, a likely assumption to make for trade cycle data.

We prefer not to discuss these matters further, primarily because Neftci, in spite of his methodological criticisms and his different method of analysis, arrives at exactly the same conclusion as all other competent investigators: "the evidence favors asymmetry".

However, we wish to make a general observation at this point: Statistical theory has become a highly developed mathematical discipline. Nonetheless, like all mathematics, its conclusions are no better (and no worse) than the initial assumptions at the start of the mathematics. Wesley Mitchell had a deep and sound scepticism concerning the application of textbook statistical methods to business cycle data, a scepticism which we share. The assumptions underlying the textbook statistical methods are rather simple, and there is no reason to believe that these assumptions apply to business cycle data. The shape of the cycle, asymmetrical as it is, should be a warning in itself. No **simple** set of statistical assumptions can give rise to such an asymmetrical shape. In dealing with data of this sort, it is dangerous to get into elaborate mathematical manipulations based on oversimple initial assumptions. Less mathematical theory, and more attention to the actual data, are very much in order.

After this digression, let us return to the data on pig iron production. The difference found by Burns and Mitchell between average upslopes and downslopes appears striking. However, to estimate the statistical significance of this difference, we need individual slope values, not merely the average slopes. Burns and Mitchell do not report these values.

We have therefore gone back to the raw data as given in Macaulay's book, [6] that is, the identical data used by Burns and Mitchell, and we have repeated the entire analysis.

The ordinate in chart 35 of Burns and Mitchell is logarithmic, and the long-term trend curve drawn there is clearly some simple curve in terms of the logarithm (rather than the natural value) of pig iron production. Let P(t) be the average daily production of pig iron in month t, with January 1877 corresponding to t=1. Let x(t) be its logarithm, x(t) = log P(t). Our fitted long term trend curve is quadratic and was obtained from a least squares fit to the values of x(t) for the years 1877 to 1929, inclusive. Our equation for the trend curve is:

```
(1)   z(t) = log T(t) = a + b*t - c*t**2
      where
      a=0.71978, b=0.00386345, c=0.0000028816
```

This curve agrees closely with the one of Burns and Mitchell. We then take the "de-trended part" of pig iron production to be represented by the quantity:

```
(2)   y(t) = x(t) - z(t) = log[P(t)/T(t)]
```

[6] Macauley 1938.

The next step is seasonal adjustment of these y-values. Pig iron production data must be adjusted seasonally, since activities using iron (railway construction, building, etc.) are influenced strongly by the weather, and with them the demand for pig iron. [7] We used method 2 of Burns and Mitchell for this seasonal adjustment. [8] By a suitable choice of parameters we were able to get results very close to the ones read off from their chart 35.

In the table below we list all turning points in our series, for the years 1879 through 1933, inclusive. In the table the slopes are given with signs, i.e. the slopes of downward phases exhibit negative signs. In the values of the means, given at the bottom of the table, signs have been ignored. [9]

The null hypothesis that the cycle is symmetric implies that the ascending slopes and the descending slopes must be drawn from the same distribution function (though we do not know the functional form of it). It is therefore appropriate to try a standard statistical test to see whether our sample of 15 ascending slopes and our sample of 15 descending slopes could come from the same underlying distribution. The Cramer-von-Mises two sample test [10] compares the empirical distribution functions of two samples. The value of the test statistic T2 is 0.617, corresponding to 98 percent significance level for the final conclusion, which is, that these data show a clear asymmetry for the cycle.

Having demonstrated the existence of asymmetry, let us discuss, briefly, the work of DeLong and Summers (DeLong 1984, 1986) purporting to prove the opposite. A detailed paper on this matter is in preparation, and we confine ourselves here to a mere list of the main points.

A. We have repeated the DeLong and Summers calculation for the "coefficient of skew" of the distribution of "growth

[7] This is merely one illustration of our earlier warning that attention to the actual data is needed, more than sophistication in mathematical statistics.
[8] Burns 1947 p.47.
[9] Our scaling differs from that of Burns 1947. Hence our slopes differ numerically, by a scale factor. The ratio of average upslope to average downslope is in good agreement.
[10] Conover 1971 p.314.

Table A.1. CYCLICAL TURNING POINTS.

Date	Value of y(t) (seasonally corrected)	Slope of preceding phase
3/79	-0.0842	
2/82	0.0989	0.00523
1/85	-0.1196	-0.00625
10/87	0.0953	0.00651
3/88	-0.0350	-0.02607
6/90	0.1269	0.00600
4/91	-0.1606	-0.02875
10/91	0.0999	0.04341
10/93	-0.3620	-0.01924
10/95	0.0444	0.01693
10/96	-0.2641	-0.02571
12/99	0.0590	0.00850
10/00	-0.1048	-0.01639
6/03	0.0892	0.00606
12/03	-0.2132	-0.05040
12/06	0.1496	0.01008
1/08	-0.2029	-0.02711
12/09	0.1656	0.01602
7/11	-0.0517	-0.01144
1/13	0.1349	0.01036
12/14	-0.1850	-0.01391
10/16	0.1429	0.01490
5/19	-0.1063	-0.00804
8/20	0.0823	0.01258
7/21	-0.4869	-0.05175
7/23	0.1242	0.02546
7/24	-0.1970	-0.02676
8/26	0.0611	0.01032
11/27	-0.0455	-0.00711
8/29	0.1007	0.00696
3/33	-0.7954	-0.02084

	Mean	Standard deviation
15 ascending slopes	0.01375	0.00925
15 descending slopes	0.02265	0.01387

rates" of United States G.N.P. [11] Our results disagree completely with theirs. They get skew values of both signs, we get, consistently, negative skew values.

B. Business cycle data are notoriously "jagged", with many, insignificant ups and downs within each cycle. A statistical analysis carried out directly on these raw data is therefore most unsatisfactory, in spite of what DeLong and Summers assert. The short term variations distort the calculated "skew" value, quite badly. Some process of "data smoothing" is essential here. When this is done, the negative skew values become more negative, as well as more consistent with each other over different time periods.

C. We do not accept that G.N.P. and other "macro" data are the most suitable vehicles for studying the trade cycle.

1. Prior to Keynes' General Theory (Keynes 1936), G.N.P. was not recognized as an economic category, and no one measured it at the time. Therefore, all pre World War II "data" are later reconstructions, based on other, by no means complete or completely relevant, evidence.
2. Post World War II data on G.N.P. do not suffer from this problem, but there is reason to believe that the trade cycle has changed its character, compared to the nineteenth and early twentieth centuries. For example, there is no post World War II counterpart of the "panics" of, for example, 1873, 1907, or 1929.
3. Investment expenditures enter into G.N.P., of course, but they are by no means the main contribution. The major cycle is thought, at least since Keynes, to be associated with fluctuations in investment. Therefore, economic quantities directly tied to real investment (such as the production of pig iron) are more suitable for trade cycle studies than G.N.P.

More can be said, and is said in our detailed paper. For the purposes of this book, there is no need to continue: **the asymmetry of the trade cycle is real, not a statistical mirage or the result of incorrect data analysis.**

[11] The data are quarterly real G.N.P., taken from the same source as used by DeLong and Summers (Gordon 1986).

APPENDIX B: Symmetry Theorems for Frisch Type Models

In this appendix to section 4C, we give a brief summary of the symmetry theorems for Frisch type models which we stated in that Section. We shall state the steps involved in the proof, but without all the mathematical detail. The purpose is not to exhibit a full proof, but rather to show the reasoning which is involved in it. The full proof can be found in Boyd (1986).

Let us now list the various steps, and discuss each one briefly.

A. "Frisch type models" are defined unambiguously. This definition (which we gave in section 4C) has three parts:

1. The "natural motion" of the system, in the absence of external shocks, must be stable, and must not itself give rise to business cycle type ups and downs.
2. The, assumed random, shocks must be sufficiently small so that the deviations from growth equilibrium caused by them can be treated to an adequate accuracy by an approximation linear in these deviations.
3. The statistical distribution of the random shocks must exhibit the following **symmetry property:** A given series of shocks, and its "reversed" series (positive shocks replaced by equal negative shocks, and vice versa), must both occur with the same probability.

If these defining properties are satisfied by the model, then we call it a "Frisch type model".

B. Rather than working directly with the raw data (for example, on production of pig iron), we make two transformations:

1. We work with the logarithm of the economic quantity (this is equivalent to the common device of plotting the quantity "on a ratio scale"). For example, if $P(t)$ is the production of pig iron in period number t, then we work, not with $P(t)$ itself, but rather with the quantity $x(t) = \log P(t)$.
2. Before any further analysis, we first "de-trend" this $x(t)$ by subtracting, from it, a smooth "trend curve" $z(t) = \log T(t)$, where the letter "T" stands for "trend". [For an example of such a trend curve on a ratio plot, see chart 35 on page 272 of Burns and Mitchell

(1947). For an example of a fitted trend curve $z(t) = \log[T(t)]$, see equation (1) of Appendix A. Note that the trend curve must be smooth, but need not be a simple exponential growth.] That is, our de-trended value is defined by:

$$y(t) = x(t) - z(t) = \log[P(t)/T(t)] \qquad (1)$$

The intuitive meaning of $y(t)$ is this: A positive $y(t)$ means that actual production $P(t)$ in period t was above the long term trend $T(t)$; a negative $y(t)$ means that actual production was below the trend value. If the trend curve has been chosen sensibly, then there should be positive as well as negative $y(t)$ values, with the average coming out close to zero.

These logarithmic and de-trended quantities $y(t)$ are our basic economic variables.

C. It can be shown that the "fluctuating parts" of Frisch type models, as defined here, are equivalent to the usual linearized models used by econometricians. Such models can be put into "state space form":

$$x(t+1) = Ax(t) + Bu(t) + q(t) \qquad (2)$$

where x is an m-component vector of endogenous variables, [1] A is a given m-by-m matrix, u is an s-vector of exogenous variables, B is a given m-by-s matrix, and q is an m-vector of random shocks, with some assumed probability distribution, for example, multi-variate Gaussian. Every linear econometric model can be put in this form. In order to simulate such a model, one must specify, in addition to the matrices A and B:

1. The exogenous variables, i.e., the s-vectors $u(t)$ at all times t.
2. The initial state of the model, i.e., the m-vector $x(0)$ at the initial time $t=0$.
3. The joint probability distribution of all the shocks $q(t)$ (i.e., for all times t, and all the m vector components of q).

---

[1] Some of the m components of this vector may be time-delayed values of other components.

D. The vector x(t) in equation (2) has not been "de-trended" as yet, and thus does not correspond to the y(t) of equation (1) as deduced from actual data. In particular, sudden changes in exogenous variables (in one or more of the components of the vector u(t)) will affect the way x(t) develops in time. Such sudden changes in exogenous variables are called "type I shocks" by Adelman and Adelman. [2] These authors have demonstrated that such shocks, of reasonable magnitude, are insufficient to explain business cycle fluctuations. It is thus permissible, and highly convenient, to ignore all type I shocks from the start, and concentrate instead on what Adelman and Adelman call "type II shocks", i.e., the effect of the random shock terms q(t) in equation (2).

E. We therefore separate out, from the actual time series x(t), an exogenously determined part z(t) and a "fluctuating" part y(t). The first of these does not involve the shocks at all, and is defined by:

$$(3) \quad z(t+1) = Az(t) + Bu(t)$$

with the initial condition

$$(4) \quad z(0) = x(0)$$

The other, fluctuating part is the one of interest to us, and is defined by:

$$(5) \quad y(t) = x(t) - z(t)$$

This y(t), derived from a standard linear econometric model, can be compared directly to the "observed" y(t) of equation 1.

F. Our definition of y(t) makes the time t=0 a bit special. However, Frisch type models (by assumption) are stable, and therefore exhibit only limited "memory" for the way in which they were started at time t=0. We exploit this property, by starting our analysis for "specific cycles" (i.e., cycles in some one particular component of the vector y(t)), not at time t=0, but at a somewhat later time, sufficiently large

[2] Adelman 1959.

so that the initial condition (4) has been "forgotten" by the model.

G. A model of the form of equation (2) produces seasonal variations, if at all, only via "seasonal dummies" among the components of the vector u(t) of exogenous variables. Since all exogenous variables have been excluded, by definition, from the "fluctuating part" y(t) of equation (5), there are no seasonal variations in y(t). Any comparison with actual data must therefore be made after some suitable seasonal adjustment of the raw data. We use the methods of the N.B.E.R. in such cases. [3]

H. Although we employ the methods pioneered by the N.B.E.R. as much as possible, we do not need to reproduce the N.B.E.R. "reference cycles", i.e., coincident cycles in many different economic variables. Our interest here is in Frisch type models, not in real business cycles. For Frisch type models, the "coupling" between different economic variables is contained in the off-diagonal elements of the matrix A, and in the non-zero elements of the matrix B, in equation (2). There is therefore no need, in a purely theoretical investigation like the present one, to identify reference cycles: they are there, whether we identify them or not, and it is much easier to work with one economic variable (one component of the vector y(t)) at a time. In N.B.E.R. terminology, this means we concern ourselves only with "specific cycles".

J. Let us now start to deduce theoretically predicted properties of y(t), by using equations (2) through (5). First of all, (5) together with (4) yields:

$$(6) \qquad y(0) = 0$$

We have mentioned this earlier, and remarked that we start our analysis at a somewhat later time, so that the special initial condition (6) will have been forgotten by the system by then. Subtracting (3) from (2) and using (5) yields the following equation for the time development of the fluctuating part y(t):

$$(7) \qquad y(t+1) = Ay(t) + q(t)$$

[3] Burns 1947 pp.36,40.

As mentioned earlier, the vector of exogenous variables u(t), and the matrix B which connects it with the rest of the system, no longer appear in this equation.

K. Next, let us show that the y(t) have expected value zero, at all times t, provided only this is true of the shocks q(t) themselves. That is, we assume:

$$(8) \qquad E[q(t)] = 0$$

where "E" stands for the expected value. Taking expected values on both sides of equation (7), we get

$$E[y(t+1)] = AE[y(t)] + 0$$

and hence, by equation (6) and mathematical induction:

$$(9) \qquad E[y(t)] = 0 \quad \text{for} \quad t = 0, 1, 2, \ldots$$

which completes the proof.

L. Let us now define precisely what we mean by the "reflection property" of a time series:

$$(10) \qquad S: \qquad y(1), y(2), \ldots, y(T)$$

extending over the time periods t = 1, 2, 3, ..., T. In a stochastic model such as equation (7), there is associated with any such realization a probability density measure P(S). The detailed determination of the measure P(S) is likely to be complicated, but we shall not need to determine it. Now let S' be the "reflected time series"

$$(11) \qquad S': \qquad -y(1), -y(2), \ldots, -y(T)$$

There is a probability measure P(S') for this reflected series, as well.

Definition: A stochastic process giving a time series y(0), y(1), ..., y(T) of vector random variables is said to have the **reflection property** if P(S) = P(S') for every realization of the time series.

M. **Theorem:** If the joint probability distribution for the shocks q(t) has the reflection property, and the time series satisfies (7) then the stochastic process y(t) also has the reflection property.

The proof of this theorem is by inspection.

N. In order to proceed to our desired conclusion, we must assume a suitable reflection property not only for the time series of shocks q(t), but also for whatever method is used to determine the turning points of the resulting time series of deviations y(t). A number of methods are conceivable for a programmed determination of turning points. In order to keep within the standard literature, we adopt the method of Bry and Boschan. [4] We remark that this method does have the **reflection property:** The same turning points are identified for a time series S and its reflected series S', with peaks becoming troughs and vice versa.

P. We are now ready to state and prove our symmetry theorems for Frisch type models:

Let y(t) be a vector time series of fluctuating variables, all of them satisfying the symmetry property. We nominate some suitable positive time, call it t0, as the starting time for our analysis. For each component of the vector y(t) separately, we determine specific cycle turning points for times t > t0. We determine exactly 2n+1 turning points, so as to cover exactly n full cycles. Each of these n cycles has an ascending phase and a descending phase. We denote the slope of the ascending phase of the k'th cycle in component i by p'(i,k). Similarly, p"(i,k) denotes the slope of the descending phase of the k'th cycle in component i, with the negative sign ignored. At times, we shall use the symbol p' to stand for all the upslopes p'(i,k), i = 1, 2, ..., m and k = 1, 2, ..., n; and similarly, we use p" to stand for all the downslopes p"(i,k). Let the probability of getting such a set of slopes be denoted by P(p',p").

Symmetry theorem: Let the stochastic vector time series y(t) have the reflection property, and let the rules used for determining specific cycle turning points for each component i of the series have its reflection property, also. Then it is true that P(p',p") is a symmetric function, i.e., for any two m-by-n matrices A and B it is true that P(A,B) = P(B,A).

Proof: Let S (equation (10)) be any realization of the time series. Determine the turning points, and hence the slopes p'(i,k) and p"(i,k) for S. Now consider the reflected time series S' (equation (11)). The exact same

[4] Bry 1971.

turning points are identified for that series, but peaks and troughs have interchanged their roles. Therefore, p'(i,k) and p"(i,k) have also been interchanged. By assumption, the probability measures of S and S' are equal. Hence these two realizations, taken together, contribute exactly equal amounts to the density functions P(p',p") and P(p",p'). Since **all** realizations of the time series can be so paired, the conclusion of the theorem follows.

Q. This theorem contains many other theorems as immediate corollaries. We are interested particularly in those corollaries which can be obtained by integrating the joint density function P(p',p") over all those slopes which involve vector components i other than some one specific component, say other than i=1. That is, we want to be able to concentrate on the analysis of cycles, and their associated upslopes and downslopes, for one particular economic quantity, without having to worry about the interrelationships which exist between this and other economic quantities.

We concentrate on component 1 (by suitable renumbering, any component can be so numbered). For convenience of notation, we let S' be the n-component vector with components p'(1,1), p'(1,2), ..., p'(1,n); that is, S' is the vector formed from all the measured upslopes of economic quantity number 1. We let S" be the n-component vector with components p"(1,1), p"(1,2), ..., p"(1,n); that is, S" contains all the downslopes for this same economic quantity. Further, denote by P(S',S") the joint probability density for these two vector variables.

Corollary 1: P(S',S") is a symmetric function, i.e., for any two n-vectors U and V, it is true that P(U,V) = P(V,U).
Proof: Take the symmetry theorem, and integrate over all the variables p'(i,k) and p"(i,k) with i different from 1.

Next, let P(S') be the joint probability density for the upslopes only, obtained by integrating P(S',S") over all the downslopes (all the components of the vector S"). Similarly, let P(S") be the joint probability density for the downslopes only, obtained by integrating P(S',S") over all the upslopes (all the components of the vector S').

Corollary 2: The two functions P(S') and P(S") have the same functional form.
Proof: Take corollary 1 and carry out the integrations.

Next, define the average upslope r'(n) and the average downslope r"(n) by

(12) r'(n) = [p'(1,1)+p'(1,2)+...+p'(1,n)]/n

(13) $r''(n) = [p''(1,1)+p''(1,2)+...+p''(1,n)]/n$

Corollary 3: The statistics $r'(n)$ and $r''(n)$ are distributed identically.
Proof: This is an immediate consequence of corollary 2.
Corollary 4: The expected values of $r'(n)$ and $r''(n)$ equal each other.
Last, consider the quantity x defined by

(14) $x = [r'(n) - r''(n)]/[r'(n) + r''(n)]$

Corollary 5: The statistic x is distributed symmetrically around x=0, and the expected value of x is zero.

R. The joint probability density P(S',S") of corollary 1 contains the possibility of correlations between all these slopes. Since most standard statistical tests for distributions work best when the trials are independent, it would help greatly to be able to ignore these correlations.

An a priori, analytic calculation of these correlations is so difficult as to be impractical. However a Monte Carlo calculation on a computer is entirely possible.

We have performed such Monte Carlo estimates of the correlations between the various slopes in models of the Frisch type. The details are much too extensive to be recounted here; we refer to Boyd (1986) for a full account. All the theoretical correlation coefficients are near zero, so near indeed that **it is an excellent approximation to ignore these correlations altogether.**

S. At this stage, the theoretical work is complete. We have clear theoretical predictions of symmetry of the cycle, after removal of long term trend components from the raw data. In particular, the upslopes (components of the vector S') and downslopes (components of the vector S") are predicted to be samples drawn from the **same distribution function.** Furthermore, the theoretically predicted correlations are sufficiently small so that they can be ignored, i.e., the separate upslopes and downslopes should behave very nearly like statistically independent variates.

Just these predictions were compared with the observations on business cycles, in section 4C and Appendix A, and have turned out to be in direct contradiction to the observations. **All Frisch type models are therefore excluded by the evidence.**

APPENDIX C: Specification of the Model

In this appendix, we have collected together the mathematical equations of our model. With each equation, we give a reference to the section, or sections, of the main text in which that equation is discussed and motivated.

THE MODEL EQUATIONS.

Equations for group 1.

Investor confidence f, related to time t and bankruptcy rate B (see section 6B for motivation and discussion):

(1) df/dt = 1 - a1*B*f

where a1 is a constant parameter. Note that f has dimension T (time), so that df/dt is dimensionless. B has dimension 1/T, hence the product Bf is dimensionless, and hence so is the parameter a1 (equal to unity in our simulation). Such dimensional checks are very valuable, and we recommend their use strongly.

Investor desired investment fraction G (see section 7B):

(2) dG/dt = a2*[1 - G*sign(D)]*D + b(G)

Here D is the fractional rate of increase of the share price index (see equation 9 below), a2 is a constant parameter, and b(G) is a "soft barrier" designed to prevent the value of G from dropping below zero. The choice of a soft, rather than a hard, barrier for dG/dt has no economic significance and is done only for technical reasons of computer programming and numerical analysis. We have taken the mathematical form of the function b(G) to be (b3 is a constant parameter of dimension 1/T):

(3) b(G) = (b3/G)*ramp(G1 - G)

where [1]

(4) $\text{ramp}(x) = x \quad \text{if } x >= 0,$
$\qquad\qquad = 0 \quad \text{if } x < 0.$

Investor perceived income flow y (see sections 7C, 8B and 8C):

(5) $y = v' + (D + j - B)*J + q$

v' is the (assumed constant) rental for the use of land, and the second term includes capital gains DJ, dividend payments jJ, and capital losses associated with bankruptcies -BJ. The dividend rate j is taken to be a constant (equal to 0.12).

The last term, q, represents the flow of new money due to gold mining, assumed (for simplicity) to go in the first instance to our group 1 (see chapter 8). The simulations shown in chapter 7 are without this term, i.e., q = 0. Simulations with positive q (q = 20) are shown in chapter 8.

Investor desired consumption (see section 7C):

(6) $c* = k'*\text{ramp}[y/(y + k")]$

where k' and k" are constant parameters. This formula "saturates" for y >> k", to a saturation level equal to k'; for y near zero the initial slope equals k'/k"; we call attention to conditions on the parameters k' and k", presented later on in this Appendix.

Investor actual consumption c (see section 7C):

(7) $dc/dt = b1*(c* - c)$

where b1 is the common adjustment rate parameter (dimension 1/T) for all "financial" processes in this model.

Flow rate of investment funds (see section 7C). G is the desired value of the investment fraction. J is the perceived value of current share holdings, A1 is the total perceived wealth of group 1. Thus the ratio J/A1 is the actual value of the investment fraction, and the flow rate L

[1] We call attention to equation E.1 (equation 1 of Appendix E), which gives the form used for numerical work.

produces a delayed adjustment of actual to desired values. The ramp function ensures that the flow of investment funds is "one-way" only.

(8) L = b1*A1*ramp[G - (J/A1)]

Share market fractional rate of change of price index D (see sections 6C and 6D). The first term on the right is the "fundamental" effect. The second term is the "immediate effect of bankruptcies". The term with coefficient b4 is the "soft barrier" effect on the movement of the share price index P. P1 is the soft barrier value, taken to be 0.8. u1 is a random shock term, of dimension 1/time and with mean value zero (see equation 20 later).

(9) D = b1*(fj - 1) - a3*B + (b4/P)*ramp(P1 - P) + u1

Share market price index P (see sections 6C and 6D). This equation is a mathematical consequence of the meaning of D, that is, D = (d/dt)(log P); the economic assumptions are contained in equation (9) for D.

(10) dP/dt = PD

Accounting identity for perceived assets of investors:

(11) d(A1)/dt = y - c

Perceived total value of outstanding shares (another accounting identity). The term L represents purchase of newly issued securities; the term DJ represents capital gains (when D is positive) or capital losses (when D is negative); the term -BJ represents capital losses associated with bankruptcies.

(12) dJ/dt = L + (D - B)J

Equations for group 2.

Failure rate B of speculative enterprises (see section 7D). u2 is a random variable of dimension 1/time, with mean value equal to zero; note that this random shock term is capable of making B non-zero even when d(A2)/dt is positive.

(13) $B = \text{ramp}[-(1/A2)(d(A2)/dt) + u2]$

Rental v" for use of capital, paid from group 3 to group 2 (see section 7E).

(14) $v'' = a4*(c + z)$

Accounting identity for cash asset position A2 of group 2 (see section 7E). Payments of dividends and/or interest to investors is taken to be jJ where J is governed by equation 12 and j is a constant, equal to 0.12 for the simulations shown here. z is the rate of expenditure on construction of new projects.

(15) $d(A2)/dt = v'' + L - z - jJ$

Desired activity level z* (see section 7E).

(16) $z^* = a5*L$

Actual activity level z (see section 7E). The first term on the right is an adjustment to the desired level, with a slow ("real") adjustment rate b2 = 0.3; the second term represents involuntary cessation of activities due to bankruptcies.

(17) $dz/dt = b2*(z^* - z) - Bz$

Equation for group 3.

Schematic accounting identity for cash asset position A3 (see section 7F). Here v' is the, assumed constant, rental for land paid to group 1, total consumption c is given by equation (7), activity level of group 2 z is given by equation (17), and rental for capital services v" by equation (14).

(18) $d(A3)/dt = c + z - v' - v''$

We note that A3 does not influence any other endogenous variable of the model.

RANDOM SHOCK TERMS.

There is a considerable body of opinion that many economic variables are subject to fluctuations which can be modelled as random walks. [2] The modelling of a random walk is fairly straight forward when the economic model uses discrete time t = 1, 2, ... For example, one random walk model of stock market prices is obtained by making the price at time t equal to the sum of the price at time t-1 and a random shock variable (with a new value at each new time t). In symbols:

$$(19) \quad P(t) = P(t-1) + U(t)$$

where U(t) is a random variable with zero mean. Granger and Morgenstern [3] show that this fits the short run behavior of stock markets fairly well, but it fails to fit the long run (longer than two years) behavior.

In continuous time, almost the entire literature approximates the shocks by so-called "white noise". In engineering, this approximation is often completely justified and reasonable. The source of the random disturbances to engineering systems is usually a series of many, very tiny, "shocks", with no one event particularly noticeable.

Ordinarily, in economics, when a model is constructed in continuous time, as ours is, random variables are also taken to be "white noise". [4] However, for shocks to speculative markets, the white noise assumption is highly suspect. Merton [5] has suggested that:

> The antipathetical process to this continuous stock price motion would be a 'jump' stochastic process defined in continuous time. In essence, such a process allows for a positive probability of a stock price change of extraordinary magnitude, no matter how small the time interval between successive observations. Indeed, since empirical studies of stock price series

[2] For example, see Granger and Morgenstern (Granger 1970), especially pp.76-77 where they discuss the history of the random walk model of stock market prices from Bachelier in 1900 onwards.

[3] Granger 1970.

[4] Samuelson 1965a, 1965b; Bergstrom 1976.

[5] Merton 1976 pp.126-127.

tend to show far too many outliers for a simple constant-variance log-normal distribution, there is a 'prima-facie' case for the existence of such jumps. On a less scientific basis, we have all observed price changes in stocks (usually in response to some announcement) which at least on the surface, appear to be 'jumps'."

The random variables in our model, u1 and u2, are modelled as Poisson jump processes. [6] In such a process, the probability of a shock is independent of the present state of the system, and of all previous states. The random shock terms we use are defined as follows:

Let r1 be a dimensionless random variable, distributed uniformly in the interval (0,1). Let rt12 = 3.464 stand for the square root of 12, and let b5 be a parameter of dimension 1/(time). The random shock variable u1, of dimension 1/time and with mean value zero, is then defined by:

(20) u1 = rt12*b5*(r1 - 0.5)

Note that the parameter b5 in equation (20) equals the root-mean-square value of u1. New values of r1 are drawn at random times, chosen so that the time intervals between drawings are distributed exponentially, with mean value equal to a parameter t1, of dimension time. Note that this parameter t1 is not an integer, but rather is a fraction of a year, in practice.

The random shock variable u2, also with mean value zero, is defined analogously by:

(21) u2 = rt12*b6*(r2 - 0.5)

where r2 is a random variable distributed uniformly in the interval (0,1). New values of r2 are drawn at random times, chosen so that the time intervals between drawings are distributed exponentially, with mean value equal to the parameter t2. Note that the parameter b6 equals the root-mean-square value of u2.

These "jumps" appear in the formulas for the variables D and B, equations (9) and (13). These variables occur on the right-hand sides of differential equations (e.g., equations 1, 2, 10, 12, 17). In consequence, all the endogenous vari-

[6] Bailey 1964 pp.67-69.

ables of the model remain continuous functions of time even when random shocks are present; although some of the endogenous variables then exhibit sudden changes of slope.

We call attention to Appendix E, equations E.2 through E.6, where u1 and u2 are redefined in a form suitable for numerical work.

CONDITIONS AND RESTRICTIONS.

The model parameters k', k" and v' can not be chosen completely independently of each other. The first two decide desired consumption c* as a function of perceived income y, the last is income from rents on land. Economically, it is reasonable to suppose that desired consumption expenditure for the case y = v' should not exceed v'. The argument runs as follows: consumption patterns of group 1 should not have altered too violently compared to an earlier period when there was rather less gambling on the money market. In that earlier period, an investor spending significantly more than his rental receipts would have soon lost his land, and thus have been eliminated as an investor.

An easy calculation shows that the condition c*(v') <= v' can be rewritten in the form:

(22) k' <= v' + k"

Our chosen parameters obey this condition.

Also of interest is the marginal propensity to consume, or more precisely, the marginal value of the desired consumption level c*. It follows from equation 6 that this equals (k'*k")/(y+k")**2. With our parameter values, this equals 0.75 when y = v', which we consider a reasonable value.

Note that a common scale factor can be employed for scaling the quantities v', k', k", and all those endogenous and auxiliary variables which are money values or value flows; such a common factor merely scales the unit of currency. Our scaling makes this unit equal to one million pounds sterling.

Several parameters have restrictions on their values, from economic reasoning or historical experience. For example, a4 in equation 14 must be positive and significantly less than unity. a5 in equation 16 must be larger than unity, but must not be excessively large. The "soft barrier" level P1 in equation 9 on the share price index P should lie below unity, [7] but not too far below. The adaptation rates b1 and b2, for "financial" and "real" investment, respectively, must be such that b1 >> b2, with 1/b2 of the order of several years.

It is the existence of a number of restrictions of this sort which mean that we can not just choose our numbers completely arbitrarily, or fit any kind of behavior whatever. Still, there is a great deal of freedom in choosing parameters. However, while it is easy to choose parameters (and/or initial values of endogenous variables) for which we get unacceptable solutions (a very common trouble is that the model economy simply "dies" after one or two crashes), there does exist a reasonably wide range of values for which the model yields solutions which are qualitatively similar to what happened in the nineteenth century trade cycle.

In this area of research, we believe, excessive ambition is self-defeating. A full exploration of all possible mathematical solutions of our system of equations, for all possible parameter values and all possible initial conditions, is simply out of the question; nor are our equations sufficiently realistic, economically, to warrant such a major mathematical investigation.

In any case, we know and admit freely that our equations are capable of generating some unreasonable and quite unacceptable solutions when one chooses poor parameter values and/or unsuitable initial values for the endogenous variables. In our opinion, this is not an important objection. These equations are, so far as we know, the **only existing model of the trade cycle which is capable of yielding qualitatively acceptable solutions.** In this, very difficult, area of non-linear modelling, we consider this a significant success.

NUMERICAL VALUES.

In this section we present numerical values of all model parameters, as well as starting values (at time t = 0) of

[7] Recall that we have taken P = 1 to represent a share market level appropriate for a market which has barely recovered from the last crash.

all endogenous variables, for the simulations shown in chapters VII and VIII.

Parameters a1 through a6 are dimensionless, b1 through b6 and j have dimension 1/(time), t1 through t4 have dimension time (in years). [8] G1 and P1 are dimensionless. v', k' and k" are value flows, in millions of pound sterling per annum.

a1 = 1	j = 0.12
a2 = 0.5	k' = 63
a3 = 2	k" = 50
a4 = 0.25	G1 = 0.01
a5 = 2	P1 = 0.8
a6 = 0.0001	t1 = 0.08
b1 = 1	t2 = 0.13
b2 = 0.3	t3 = 20
b3 = 3	t4 = 0.01
b4 = 3	v' = 15

b5 = 0.32, or = 0 for figures 7.1B-7.4B
b6 = 0.24, or = 0 for figures 7.1B-7.4B

The model used has very few variables which are not endogenous: the time t, the random shocks u1 and u2, and gold production q. The last of these, q, the only truly exogenous variable, has been set equal to zero in the simulations shown in figures 7.1-7.4. q has been set equal to 20 (20 million pounds sterling per annum) in the alternative simulations of chapter 8.

We conclude this section by presenting starting values (nominal time t = 0) of all endogenous variables of the model, for the deterministic simulations shown in chapter VII.

A1(0) = 150	c(0) = 18	J(0) = 18
A2(0) = 15	f(0) = 10	P(0) = 1.00
A3(0) = 60	G(0) = 0.15	z(0) = 2.2

With these starting values for endogenous variables, and a suitable differential equation solution package, our computer solution can be reproduced. We call attention, however, to the contents of Appendix E which should be studied carefully before attempting this.

[8] The parameters a6, t3 and t4 appear in the changes required for numerical work. They are introduced in appendix E.

APPENDIX D: **Impossibility of Balanced Growth**

In this appendix we will produce some partial solutions to the differential equations given in Appendix C. We assert that this model is incapable of balanced exponential growth even in the presence of gold mining. We will now demonstrate and discuss this.

We shall find that any simple exponential growth solution is eliminated by our mechanism of business confidence and investment evaluation. With confidence and share prices governed as they are in our model, confidence grows continually in a period of prosperity. As a result share prices also grow continually, and the total market value of an investment portfolio grows **at a rate much faster than simple exponential growth.** This wild rate of growth cannot be sustained by the rest of the economy, and **must** therefore result in a crash.

Note that this rate of growth occurs in spite of the fact that our confidence variable is assumed to grow at a mere linear rate, i.e. $df/dt = 1$ in the absence of bankruptcies.

Let us now proceed with the mathematical proof of these statements. We shall ignore the random shock terms u1 and u2, in equations C.9 and C.13 respectively. [1] These terms can be shown to make no qualitative difference to the argument (basically, once the supposed balanced growth is well under way, the random shock terms are too small to matter), and their omission simplifies the discussion.

Firstly, on a growth path, or in a stationary state, $d(A2)/dt >= 0$. This means that our failure rate formula (C.13) gives $B = 0$. [2]

With zero failure rate, equation (C.1) becomes $df/dt = 1$ so that

(1) $f = f0 + t$

---

[1] Equation C.9 means equation (9) of appendix C.

[2] In more elaborate models, **in the complete absence of external shocks**, there may exist purely mathematical, formal "solutions" in which the model economy is "balanced on a knife edge" in such a way that the bankruptcy rate B is non-zero but constant in time. Such "solutions" are unstable and cease to be solutions as soon as shocks are introduced.

where f0 is a constant, equal to the value of f at time t = 0. [3]

Inserting equation (1) into equation (C.9) for D, we get

(2) D = b1*[(f0 + t)*j - 1] + (b4/P)*ramp(P1-P) + u1

The average value of u1 is zero, and thus this "random walk" term has only minor effects in the long run, and we may ignore it for our present purposes. The dividend rate j is taken to be a positive constant in our model. Thus, for large enough t, the entire right hand side of equation 2 is positive. [4] When D is greater than 0, equation (C.10) gives dP/dt > 0. Therefore no matter where we start, P eventually becomes greater than P1 and thereafter we can drop the barrier term. Consequently, also, the existence, or form, of this barrier is not relevant to our proof.

For simplicity we will define two constants:

(3a) k = b1*(j*f0 - 1)
(3b) K = (b1*j)/2

Dropping all but the first term on the right side of (2), and using the definitions (3), we get:

(4) D = k + 2*K*t

We substitute this result (valid during a continued time of prosperity, possibly after waiting for some initial interval of time) into the differential equation (C.10). The resulting equation can be solved directly to yield:

(5) P(t) = P(0)*exp[k*t + K*t**2]

This result indicates a violent (much faster than simple exponential) rise of the share price index P in this model economy. From its definition, the constant K is positive (its value in our simulations is 0.06), and hence the quad-

[3] If df/dt should be any positive constant, not necessarily unity, the subsequent argument still follows through with only trivial changes.

[4] For t > [(1/j) - f0], the terms in b1 and b4 are both non-negative, so from that time on, only the random term u1 can go negative at all, and this term is eventually unable to outweigh the other two.

ratic term $K*t**2$ in the exponent dominates eventually, for t greater than k/K (after a few years).

Now consider equation (C.12) for the total share holdings J of group 1. In the absence of failures (B = 0) this becomes:

$$(6)\quad dJ/dt = L + D*J >= (k + 2*K*t)*J$$

where the inequality on the right follows from equation (4) and from L >= 0 (itself a consequence of equation (C.8)). Inequality (6) leads to:

$$(7)\quad J(t) >= J(0)*exp[k*t + K*t**2]$$

Thus, during an upswing total share valuation J grows faster than exp(K*t**2). A few moments with a calculator will show how prodigiously fast this rate of growth becomes.

This is our important point, which negates any hope of a steady balanced growth path, as neither the real quantities nor the money supply can possibly sustain this sort of growth. Eventually we must get a breakdown. Notice that we have only used a very few of the equations and assumptions of our model to arrive at this conclusion.

Qualitatively, one may put it like this: Inflows to speculative industries are limited by the ability of other groups to invest, but expectations of returns from speculation are largely psychological and the sky is the limit. Thus speculative valuations, and the consequential dividend payments, are bound to outrun, sooner or later, the available resources of the speculative entrepreneurs. Our very crude equations do lead to this result, in a striking fashion. We have thus shown that a steady state or exponential growth path are **impossible** within our model, by using only an absolute minimum of the assumptions and equations of the model.

APPENDIX E: **Computer Simulation Method**

In this chapter we shall outline the method we use for solving the equations of the model numerically on an electronic computer. For given initial values of the endogenous variables, given exogenous variables and given parameters, the computer produces numerical values for the endogenous variables obeying the equations of appendix C at various suitably spaced points within a specified time interval. This method is slow and yields only particular solutions, not general theorems. However it has the virtue that it is generally applicable to nonlinear models.

SMOOTHING OF THE EQUATIONS.

In order to use standard numerical methods for the solution of a coupled system of ordinary differential equations, it is necessary that the right-hand sides be well-behaved functions of all the endogenous variables, preferably analytic functions but at a minimum five times differentiable functions (five times for the Runge-Kutta fourth order method). This is not the case for the equations listed in appendix C, because of the function ramp(x) and the function sign(D). If random shock terms are present, then their (assumed) sudden "jumps" also interfere with the standard numerical integration methods, so that these jumps must also be smoothed.

To overcome these problems, replace the function ramp(x), wherever it occurs, by the following:

(1) $\quad \text{quiz}(x) = a6*\log[1 + \exp(x/a6)]$

where a6 is a parameter with value 0.0001 in our simulations. For x >> a6 this reduces effectively to x, while for x << -a6 it is very close to zero; thus quiz(x) reproduces the behavior of the function ramp(x) everywhere except within a distance a6 of the origin. In this latter region, quiz(x) smoothes over the sharp corner in ramp(x).

The function sign(D) in equation C.2 is replaced by tanh(t3*D), where tanh denotes the hyperbolic tangent function and t3 is a parameter of dimension time, whose value we have taken to be 20 in our simulations. Witn this choice, the function tanh(t3*D) is very close to sign(D) whenever the absolute value of D exceeds 0.1.

Finally, in the case of stochastic simulations, we need a series of definitions to smooth out the sharp, sudden jumps of the idealized Poisson process defined in appendix C. We start by defining a smoothed step function of time, with a smoothing time parameter t4 which we take to equal 0.01 years: The value t4 = 0.01 years = 3.65 days implies that the "sudden jumps" of the idealized Poisson process take this much time to develop in the real market. This is entirely reasonable. The definition of our smoothed step function reads:

(2) smstep(t) = 1/[1 + exp(-t/t4)]

We use this to define a smooth function which is close to unity for tlow < t < thigh, and close to zero for all other values of t:

(3) hump(t,tlow,thigh) = smstep(t-tlow)*smstep(thigh-t)

Next, let t(i,j) be the j'th random time point chosen from the Poisson process for random shock u(i). We define the index j(i,t) as that value of j for which t(i,j) < t <= t(i,j+1).

We are now ready to write down the smoothed version of equation C.20, which is:

(5) u1 = rt6*b5*sum[(r1(k)-0.5)*hump(t,t(1,k),t(1,k+1))]

where the "sum" extends from k = j(1,t)-3 to k = j(1,t)+3. Formula C.21 is replaced by:

(6) u2 = rt6*b6*sum[(r2(k)-0.5)*hump(t,t(2,k),t(2,k+1))]

where the "sum" extends from k = j(2,t)-3 to k= j(2,t)+3. Though unsuitable for hand computation, these formulas are no problem for a computer.

NUMERICAL INTEGRATION METHOD.

The solution of our equations involves rapid and violent changes in some of the endogenous variables. In particular f, our indicator of investment confidence, is expected to large part of the time, during the long slow recovery from the panic, the variables change only slowly.

Because of the rapid rate of change of some variables during the panic phase, the solution must be calculated at closely spaced points during this phase. This close spacing is inappropriate during the recovery phase, since

1. The computer takes excessive time in calculating the solution, leading to very costly simulation runs.
2. The large number of computations required increases the effect of rounding errors accumulating, thus limiting the accuracy of the solution severely.

Therefore, an essential requirement of any acceptable method is a **variable step size.** That is, our method must estimate the error caused by discretization for each step [1] and if necessary reduce the step size, repeating calculations in which too much error was found, until a satisfactory level of error is achieved. On the other hand, if the error per step is well below our requirements, an increase in the stepsize can and should be made.

Numerical analysis textbooks devote considerable space to the question of the stability of numerical methods for solving differential equations. The term "instability" here denotes the excessive growth of errors as the solution proceeds, due to the nature of the method of discretizing the equations. We must select a method which exhibits stability over as wide a range as possible.

We have chosen to solve the differential equations by the Runge-Kutta-Merson method (Fox 1962), with step size adjusted automatically to retain a desired level of precision of the solution. The Merson technique suffers from the defect that the error estimate may be overconservative, i.e., may overestimate the actual error quite badly. As against this, the technique is easy to use, and the only drawback is that one may be committed to an unnecessarily small stepsize for some of the integrations.

The simulations were done on a VAX, and a typical simulation for 90 years into the future took less than 20 minutes of computer time, usually considerably less than this.

---

[1] Methods exist which develop an error estimate over several steps. This would be too slow in changing step for us.

In addition we used another indication of an inappropriate step size. This indication proved necessary, especially in handling the sudden change in the nature of the G equation when the barrier is reached (see equations C.2 and C.3). If we approach the lower barrier to G with a step size larger than the width of the barrier (0.01) then in the course of calculating the next step, the right hand sides of the equations may be evaluated with G negative, which is prohibited. We have therefore put into our program a requirement that if any variable assumes a prohibited value, the program backs up and repeats the step with a smaller step size.

A word of warning is in order for anyone trying to reproduce our deterministic simulation results from the data given here. If you employ a standard differential equation package, it is essential to make sure that this package satisfies our criteria, especially a flexible stepsize, rather than one fixed in advance. We did not use a package but did our own programming throughout, in FORTRAN. Our code is available on request, but has not been beautified for general use.

References

Adelman, I. and F., "The Dynamic Properties of the Klein-Goldberger Model", Econometrica vol.27(4), 596-625, October 1959.

American Economic Association, "Readings in Business Cycle Theory" George Allen and Unwin Ltd, 1950.

Bagehot, Walter, "Lombard Street - A Description of the Money Market", Kegan Paul, London 1873; reprinted 1962 by Richard D Irwin Inc. Homewood, Illinois.

Bailey, N.T.J., "The Elements of Stochastic Processes", Wiley, New York, 1964.

Bergstrom, A.R. (ed), "Statistical Inference in Continuous Time Economic Models", North Holland, Amsterdam 1976.

Blatt, J.M., "On the Econometric Approach to Business Cycle Analysis", Oxford Economic Papers vol.30, 292-300, 1978 (1).

Blatt, J.M., "On the Frisch Model of Business Cycles", Oxford Economic Papers vol.32(3), 467-479, 1980.

Blatt, J.M., "Dynamic Economic Systems - A Post-Keynesian Approach", M.E.Sharpe, Armonk, New York 1983.

Boschan, Charlotte - see Bry 1971, Zarnovitz 1972.

Boyd, Ian, "A Mathematical Model of the Business Cycle", Ph.D. thesis, University of New South Wales, Sydney, Australia 1986.

Brealey, Richard and Myers, Stewart, "Principles of Corporate Finance" McGraw Hill International, New York 1981.

Bry, Gerhard and Boschan, Charlotte "Cyclical Analysis of Time Series: Selected Procedures and Computer Programs (Technical Paper 20) N.B.E.R., New York 1971.

Burns, Arthur F. and Mitchell, Wesley C., "Measuring Business Cycles", N.B.E.R., New York 1947.

Cassel, G. - see Pigou 1924.

Clark, John Maurice, "Business Acceleration and the Law of Demand: A Technical Factor in Economic Cycles", Journal of Political Economy, Vol 25, 217-235, 1917.

Clemence, R.V. - see Hansen 1953.

Collier, P., and Horowitz, D., "The Rockefellers", Holt, Rinehart and Winston, New York 1976.

Conover, William Jay, "Practical Non-Parametric Statistics", Wiley, New York 1971.

Deane, P. - see Mitchell 1962.

DeLong, J. Bradford, and Summers, Lawrence H., "Are Business Cycles Symmetric?", N.B.E.R. Working Paper no. 1444, September 1984.

DeLong, J. Bradford, and Summers, Lawrence H., "Are Business Cycles Symmetric?", in Gordon 1986, pp.166-179.

Evans, D. Morier, "The Commercial Crisis 1847-1848", first published by Letts, Son and Steer, London 1848, reprinted 1969 Augustus M. Kelly, New York.

Fox, L., "Numerical Solution of Ordinary and Partial Differential Equations", Pergamon, New York 1962.

Frisch, Ragnar, "Propagation Problems and Impulse Problems In Dynamic Economics", Economic Essays in Honor of Gustav Cassell, Allen and Unwin, London 1933 pp.171-205.

Galbraith, J.K., "Money, Whence It Came, Where It Went" Andre Deutsch, London 1975.

Galbraith, J.K., "The Great Crash 1929", Hamish-Hamilton, London 1955; reprinted by Penguin, Hammondsworth, Middlesex 1975.

Giffen, R., "The Liquidations of 1973-76" in his Essays on Finance, George Bell and Sons, Fourth Edition 1886.

Goldsmith, Raymond W., "Comment on Minsky's Financial Instability Hypothesis" in Kindleberger 1982, 41-43.

Goodwin, R.M., "A Nonlinear Theory of The Cycle", Review of Economic Analysis Vol.32(4), 316-320, 1950.

Goodwin, R.M., "The Nonlinear Accelerator and the Persistence of Business Cycles", Econometrica January 1951 (4D); reprinted in Goodwin 1982.

Goodwin, R.M., "The Problem of Trend and Cycle", Yorkshire Bulletin of Economic and Social Research, August 1953, 89-97 (4D).

Goodwin, R.M., "A Model of Cyclical Growth" in "The Business Cycle in the Post War World", E. Lumberg (ed), MacMillan, London 1955, pp.203-221; reprinted in Goodwin 1982.

Goodwin, R.M., "A Growth Cycle", published in "Socialism, Capitalism and Economic Growth", Feinstein C.H. (ed) Cambridge University Press, Cambridge

1967, pp.54-58; reprinted in Goodwin 1982.
Goodwin, R.M., "A Growth Cycle", published in "A Critique of Economic Theory", E.K. Hunt and Jesse G. Schwartz (eds), Penguin, New York 1972, pp.442-449.
Goodwin, R.M., "Essays in Economic Dynamics", MacMillan, London 1982.
Gordon, Robert J., "Business Cycles: Continuity and Change", Univ. of Chicago Press, Chicago, Ill. USA 1986; see the data appendix.
Gower, L.C.R., "Principles of Modern Company Law", Stevens and Sons, London 1969.
Granger, C.W.J. and Morgenstern, O., "Predictability of Stock Market Prices", Heath and Company, Lexington, Massachusetts, 1970.
Hansen, A.H. and Clemence, R.V., "Readings in Business Cycles and National Income", George Allen and Unwin, London 1953.
Harrod, Sir Roy F., "An Essay in Dynamic Theory", Econ. Journal, vol.49, 14-33, March 1939; reprinted in Hansen (1953).
Harrod, Sir Roy F., "Towards a Dynamic Economics", MacMillan, London 1948.
Hawtrey, R.G., "A Century of Bank Rate", Longmans Green, London 1938.
Hickman, B.G., "Econometric Models Of Cyclical Behavior", N.B.E.R., Columbia University Press, New York 1972 (2 Vols).
Hicks, J.R., "A Contribution to the Theory of the Trade Cycle", Oxford University Press, Oxford 1950.
Horowitz, D. - see Collier 1976.
Hyndman, H.M., "Commercial Crises of the Nineteenth Century", Swan, Sonnenschein and Co., London 1892.
Jenks, L.H., "The Migration of British Capital to 1870", Thomas Nelson and Sons, London, 1963.
Jonson, P. (editor), "Conference on Applied Economic Research", Reserve Bank of Australia, Sydney, Australia, December 1977.
Josephson, Matthew, "The Robber Barons", Harcourt, Brace and Co., New York 1934.
Kemeny, J.G., Morgenstern, O., and Thompson, G.L., "A Generalisation of the Von Neumann Model of an Expanding Economy", Econometrica vol.24, 115-135, 1956.
Keynes, J.M., "The General Theory of Employment Interest and Money", MacMillan, London 1936 (reprinted 1976).
Keynes, J.M., "The General Theory of Employment", Quarterly Journal of Economics, Vol.51, 209-223, 1937.
Kindleberger, Charles P., and Laffargue, Jean-Pierre, "Financial Crises, Theory, history, policy", Cambridge University Press, Cambridge 1982.
Knight, Frank H., "Risk, Uncertainty and Profit", Hart, Schaffner and Marx, New York 1921.
Kondratiev, N.D., "The World Economy and its Condition During and After the War" (in Russian), Vologda p.242, 1922.
Krueger, Michael, "Aspekte einer Theorie zyklischer Kapitalsakkumulation", P. D. Lang, Frankfurt am Main, 1982.
Laffargue, Jean-Pierre - see Kindleberger 1982.
Lavington, M.A., "The Trade Cycle", P.S. King and Son, London 1922.
Lloyd, H.D., "Wealth against Commonwealth", Harper, New York 1894.
Macauley, F.R., "The Movement of Interest Rates, Bond yields, and Stock Prices in the United States since 1856", N.B.E.R., New York 1938.
Marshall, A., "Changes in the Purchasing Power of Money", in "The Economics of Industry", MacMillan, London 1879, pp.150-157, reprinted in Hansen and Clemence 1953.
Marx, Karl, "Capital vol.I", German edition Otto Meisner, Hamburg 1867, first English edition Swan, Sonnenschein, Lowey and Co., London 1887, reprinted by Progress Publishers, Moscow, 1954.
Matthews, R.C.O., "The Trade Cycle", James Nisbett and Co and Cambridge University Press, Cambridge 1959.
Mathias, Peter, "The First Industrial Nation - An economic history of Britain 1700-1914", Methuen, London 1969.
May, Robert M., "Stability and Complexity of Model Ecosystems", Princeton Univ. Press, Princeton 1973.
Meade J.E., "The Growing Economy", George Allen and Unwin Ltd, London 1968.
Merton, R.C., "Option Pricing When Underlying Stock Returns are Discontinuous", Journal of Financial Economics, Vol.3, 125-144, 1976.
Metzler, L., "The Nature and Stability of Inventory Cycles", Review of Economics and Statistics, Vol.23, 113-129, 1941.

Metzler, L., "Business Cycles and the Modern Theory of Employment", American Economic Review, Vol.36, 278-291, 1946.
Metzler, L., "Factors Governing the Length of Inventory Cycles", Review of Economics and Statistics, Vol.29, 1-15, 1947.
Metzler, L., "Three Lags in The Circular Flow of Income", 1948, in "Income, Employment, and Public Policy: Essays in Honor of Alvin Hansen" by L.A. Metzler and others, Norton, New York 1964, pp.11-32.
Mill, John Stuart, "Principles Of Political Economy", Longmans Green Reader and Dyer, London 1876.
Minsky, Hyman P., "John Maynard Keynes" Columbia University Press, New York, 1975.
Minsky, Hyman P., "The Financial Instability Hypothesis: an interpretation of Keynes and an alternative to standard theory", Nebraska Journal of Economics and Business, Vol.16(1), pp.5-16, Winter 1977.
Minsky, Hyman P., "The financial instability hypothesis: capitalist processes and the behavior of the economy" in Kindleberger 1982.
Mitchell, Wesley - see Burns 1947.
Moore, G.H. - see Zarnovitz 1972.
Morgenstern, Oskar - see Granger 1970, Kemeny 1956.
Mulhall M. "Dictionary of Statistics", George Rutledge and Sons, London 1892.
Myers, Stewart - see Brealey 1981.
Neftci, Salih N, (1984) "Are Economic Time Series Asymmetric Over The Business Cycle?", J. Political Economy, vol.92, 307-328, 1984.
Partington, John, "Railroad Purchasing and the Business Cycle", The Brookings Institution, Washington 1929.
Pigou, A.C., Cassel, G. and others "Is Unemployment Inevitable?", MacMillan, London 1924.
Pigou, A.C., "Industrial Fluctuations", MacMillan, London 1927.
Rau, N., "Trade Cycles, Theory and Evidence", MacMillan, London 1974.
Renton, G.A. (ed), "Modelling The Economy", Heinemann, London 1975.
Robinson, Joan, "The Accumulation of Capital", MacMillan, London 1956.
Rostow, W.W., "British Economy Of The Nineteenth Century" Oxford University Press, Oxford 1948.
Samuelson, Paul A., "Interaction between the Multiplier Analysis and the Principle of Acceleration", Review of Economics and Statistics, vol.21, 75-78, May 1939.
Samuelson, Paul A., "A Synthesis of the Principle of Acceleration and the Multiplier", J. Political Economy, vol.47(6), 786-797, 1939.
Samuelson, Paul A., "Rational theory of warrant pricing", Industrial Management Review, Vol.6, 13-31, 1965.
Samuelson, Paul A., "Proof that properly anticipated prices fluctuate randomly", Industrial Management Review, Vol.6, 41-49, 1965.
Schumpeter, Joseph, "Business Cycles" (2 vols.), McGraw Hill, New York, 1939.
Shackle, G.L.S., "Keynesian Kaleidics", Edinburgh University Press, Edinburgh 1974.
Summers, Lawrence J. - see DeLong 1984, 1986.
Tarbell, Ida, "History of the Standard Oil Company", New York 1904.
Thompson, G. L. - see Kemeny 1956.
Von Neumann, J., "A Model of General Economic Equilibrium", Review of Economic Studies, vol.13, 1-9, 1945.
Zarnovitz, V., Boschan, C. and Moore, G.H. "Business Cycle Analysis and Econometric Model Simulations", in Hickman 1972.
Zarnowitz, V., "The Business Cycle Today", Columbia Univ. Press, New York 1972.

Index

MIX
Papier aus verantwortungsvollen Quellen
Paper from responsible sources
FSC® C105338

If you have any concerns about our products,
you can contact us on
ProductSafety@springernature.com

In case Publisher is established outside the EU,
the EU authorized representative is:
Springer Nature Customer Service Center GmbH
Europaplatz 3, 69115 Heidelberg, Germany

Printed by Libri Plureos GmbH
in Hamburg, Germany